Guerrilla Working

Make the most of your talent by breaking the link between where you work and what you do.

Phil Jackman

To all the interesting people that I have met and the ones I have yet to.

Contents

Introduction

When I hear the word guerrilla, that iconic image of Che Guevara comes to mind with his wild beard, trade mark beret and determined stare out towards a brighter future (and with a cigar of course). The word conjures up images of small groups of soldiers emerging from the steamy jungle to engage in fierce skirmishes only for them to disappear back into the undergrowth as soon as the fighting stops.

But the word has come to have other meanings. It is often used to describe how small groups of people come together to challenge the rules and achieve positive things in a short space of time. Guerrilla gardening is a good example, a movement which sets out to use small plots of derelict land for cultivation. The word implies passion, speed and low cost.

Guerrilla marketing is another, where low-cost unconventional means are used to promote products or ideas. The word also creates an image of something out of the ordinary, a little daring perhaps but certainly exciting and fun.

And it is in this context that I have thought about this book. How can you use guerrilla like tactics to add passion, excitement and fun to business at pace and at low cost?

Through the following chapters I am going to describe how Guerrilla Working can become a reality by mixing up the people, involving the best of all of the talents to get stuck in and get back out again before everyone becomes too bogged down.

Wearing a beret isn't essential but if it helps then be my guest.

Blog entry: Guerrilla working

This is the blog that gave me the idea for this book[1].

I'd been having such fun getting in amongst my colleagues and learning about the opportunities that were out there to improve our business and one evening when I got home the concept of Guerrilla Working leapt into my head:

Modern ways of working became flexible working which begat agile working. Yet decades later we're still stuck with much of the rigid office format that we were supposed to leave behind. Yes there is now more open plan with less restricting walls yet glass partitions still mark out the work pens from the communal spaces. We have break out areas, hoteling points, touch down stations and even creative areas filled with bean bags and gaming zones but for the majority of office based workers life has not moved on that significantly.

Most travel to the same place, sit at the same desk and perform the same kinds of tasks day in and day out. The cultural shift away from the rigid work structure has just not happened as promised or expected.

The technology is there though. Laptops, tablets and smartphones with

---

[1] http://philjackman.wordpress.com/

wireless connections and long battery life connected to remotely hosted applications mean that work can be truly liberated from a single place. Add to this internet protocol telephony and follow me printing and there is no excuse.

Apart from one that is - people. Not everyone is comfortable with this type of approach. Some need to see their employees to know that they are working; indeed some need to be watched. Others feel more comfortable when they can see their boss. It is a set up that they can understand. It is what they are used to. It works and so why change?

Then there is the unmeasurable benefit of the corridor or water cooler conversation. Agile working can take away such chance meetings that are the life blood of an organisation.

Work isn't a place you go, it's a thing you do, or is it? For many the act of going somewhere, to be part of a physical group and to share time and space with your colleagues defines work. Having a common aim, a shared experience and even a mutual enemy can give a sense of purpose to who you are. So people like to go to their place of work to be with people.

But how many people when asked what they do give the building they attend rather than their job role? There is no reason why work cannot be liberated from the fixed space and still be social. Indeed work should be centred on people and not location. Working relationships should be long term but work tasks may be short.

We need a new paradigm that brings people together to work on issues, solution and opportunities only to disperse when the task is completed or another requirement is created. We need to create a much more fluid and agile approach but this will require managers and workers to let go, trust each other more and give it a try.

And that is where we come in. There are many of us who work this way already and we need to show the path and lead even more by example. We need to take the opportunity to work in places we've never tried before, in places we don't normally go to and in departments where we don't normally work. This will prove to everyone that it does work and it will help us to know more about the people we work with. Just turn up unannounced, ask if the desk is free today, open up your laptop and get going.

We need to be Guerrilla Workers. #guerrillaworking

A few myths

If you work in an office and sit behind the same desk everyday surrounded by papers, accoutrements and other paraphernalia and you think that you need them I have news for you – you don't.

If you believe that what you do requires you to be more or less in the same place performing the same tasks day in day out then you are mistaken.

You don't need your own desk. You don't need your own office. Your organisation doesn't even need a headquarters (ask Accenture).

What you need is a team of people to work with and customers to use your products or services.

But above all you need ideas.

Painting the picture

I was never very good at history when I was at school but let's start with a look back.

Work has changed enormously since when I started. In the last thirty years or so the rise of information technology has had a dramatic effect on the way that we interact, transact and communicate. Even the way we work has changed. For many of us work today is done on a screen, paying bills, designing products or writing copy. Those who still make things, those who transform base materials into usable objects tend to do so using computer enabled machinery.

But the technical transformation has just started. Who knows where this journey will take us. The rise of social media for example allows us to live our lives online, create friendships across the globe and draw on the sum of all human intellect, instantly. There are more people connected through information technology now than were alive when I was born. This mind-blowing statistic must mean that our lives have changed inexorably and new patterns of work and leisure will and already are emerging.

Yet for many of us the way that we go about our work hasn't changed much at all. We still get up, have breakfast and make our way to our place of work. There are more cars, we travel further and spend more time commuting than previous generations yet there is still a rush hour. Most of us start in the morning and finish later in the afternoon and spend the vast majority of our time within the four walls of our offices before struggling back home again.

Delyth Harris, Cisco Head of Borderless Networks Marketing[2], Europe, says that 'Work is a thing you do, not a place you go' but is it? When most people are asked what they do for a living they normally volunteer their job title rather than where they go yet their place of work is as much a determinant of their output as their job role.

Cisco's report states that 3 out of 5 workers around the world could be as productive working away from their offices as working in them. There is a disconnect however between what employees want to do or feel capable of doing and what their employers will allow and it is ironic though that a lot of work is still done at home outside of normal hours.

There have been calls for a different way of working for many years. Terminology has changed with time. Mobile working, flexible working, modern ways of working and agile working have all been in vogue and much has been promised on the back of their introduction but reality has rarely lived up to the dream.

Why is this so? Primarily because the focus has been on financial savings through the better management of physical assets rather than what is really important. Enabling employees to work from home would lead to a reduced need for office space. Couple this with a smaller individual footprint and a break from the 1:1 ratio of desk to worker and organisations could free up capital and reduce revenue costs by selling off expensive buildings.

Professor John Seddon, Managing Director of Vanguard Consulting and a leading proponent of systems thinking says however that 'The truth is counterintuitive: focusing on costs [in your business] drives costs up'.[3]

---

[2] http://newsroom.cisco.com/dlls/2010/ts_101910.html

In the same way focusing on buildings make the physical asset more important than the problem that you set out to solve.

Good buildings don't automatically lead to good businesses. It is more likely to be true the other way round. Most businesses start with what is available, either at home, in some ready built light industrial unit or a purpose built incubator building. Only when an organisation is able to stand properly on its own two feet and has reached the point that it has outgrown its first building will it look to choose the kind of place that it wants to locate. Proximity to markets and the proprietor's home are much more likely to influence the choice of building at the start.

Buildings need to be appropriate for the needs of the organisation and bear a relationship with its overall intentions, the image that it wishes to portray and its proximity to its customers.

A bank for example may feel that it needs a prestigious building in the City of London in order to exude confidence to customers and shareholders while having a tangible asset which will hold its value and that is close to where the financial action is. A software development company may take a different approach and be based in a campus style building, surrounded by amenities and have areas set aside that are fun in order to attract the kind of employees it needs and to project a youthful and slightly off the wall image.

On the other hand a public authority will want to locate its administration activities in buildings that are practical but not ostentatious and that won't incur the wrath of the tax paying public. Its democratic centre however, the council chamber for example will need to spell out the authority's place in the history of the borough and lend an air of gravitas to the important decisions that will take place within its hallowed walls.

Sir Andrew Turnbull, Cabinet Secretary and Head of the Home Civil

---

[3]http://www.nesta.org.uk/blogs/systemic_innovation_a_discussion_series/syst ems_failure_and_systems_thinking

Service, May 2004 said in 'Working without Walls[4]' that his 'own experience, as the champion of the Treasury redevelopment project, confirms there are tangible benefits to be gained from workplace and organisational change. The Treasury project illustrates vividly the way the geography of an organisation can reinforce its culture and its management aims. Through the new building we have managed to create a sense of a modern, outward looking department, an organisation with an appetite for change. The building has developed a sense of inclusiveness, breaking down traditional hierarchy. It has promoted communication, both formal and informal and has encouraged flexible ways of working. Above all it has fostered a feeling of self-confidence and presented an attractive image to the talent we need to recruit'.

The report goes on to say that 'the workplace can either support or hinder day-to-day operations, as well as help the process of change and improvement' but organisations are not bricks and mortar, glass and steel, they are built by people, run by people for the benefit of people.

Indeed there are examples where open plan office working is said to have reduced productivity. Diane Hoskins, of Gensler, an integrated architecture, design, planning and consulting firm found that knowledge work consists of four modes: focus (individual work involving concentration and attention devoted to a particular task), collaboration (working with another person or group to achieve a goal), learning (acquiring knowledge of a subject or skill through education or experience) and socialising (interactions that create trust, common bonds and values, collective identity and productive relationships).[5]

Their belief is that all types of work relied on the other but that focus was the most important. Being able to concentrate on what you are

---

[4] http://www.civilservice.gov.uk/wp-content/uploads/2012/04/Working-without-Walls.pdf

[5] http://www.smh.com.au/business/how-hotdesking-offices-can-wreck-productivity-20131229-301lh.html#ixzz2vO6urTQy

doing is the most significant factor in workplace effectiveness and an open plan environment was detrimental to making this happen.

If all types of work are dependent upon each other the how is focus the most important? Is all work equal but some more equal than others?

My own view is that we do three things: work which requires us to be with our team; work which requires us to be with our customers and; work that can be done anywhere. Guerrilla Working allows us to address all three types. It enables us to be amongst our team when needed, with our customers when beneficial and to work wherever is appropriate. If some of our work can be done anywhere then that is the place to do it.

Different approaches to working have not delivered as expected as they have focussed on the building or on the process and not on the needs of people. A different approach is needed, one which starts with the needs of the employees and the customers. As Ade McCormack asks, 'Are employee experiences more important than customer experiences? Without talent you have no business.'[6]

The 'Working without walls' report also notes that 'Experts in the world of managing culture change are quick to agree that workplace-related change can be one of the most difficult fields of organisational transformation. As a result it is often handled badly, miss-timed or even avoided. The problems are exacerbated by issues of emotional 'comfort' and 'personal ownership' which are often attached to existing environments, even when they are outdated, ineffective and inappropriate.

Of course there are some notably successful flexible working projects. Wokingham Borough Council[7] for example has introduced a project initially around cost savings and property reduction. It soon became clear however that Smart Working could tick a number of their

---

[6] http://www.ademccormack.com/
[7] http://www.wokingham.gov.uk/

corporate boxes. Their main aims were to improve the work / life balance (if such a thing exists), with 'work' being in many cases not place dependent, realise financial savings by introducing a 2:1 desk policy that would allow a rationalisation of accommodation and generate revenue from vacated space that could potentially be rented to third parties. Aligned to this was a target to reduce storage, mainly of paper records by 50%.

The project focussed heavily on the people aspects of the change developing management training courses on managing Smart Workers, employee e-learning modules about working remotely and the intranet where lots of practical advice and tips were held on protocols, policies, technology etc. It expected people to follow some basic principles:

- Be customer focused
- Accessible
- Flexible, adaptable and resilient
- Strong performance management
- Management by outputs
- Be more efficient through the use of technology.

Their own narrative adds 'So far nearly 300 people have moved to Smart Working, about a third of the overall target audience. There have been both financial and people-related achievements to date'.

BT has used the power of flexible working to stay competitive and responsive. The BT Workstyle project is available to almost everyone in the group and there are over 70,000 flexible workers, from senior managers to contact centre staff.

Sir Christopher Bland[8], Chairman of BT Group between May 2001 and September 2007 said, "At BT, flexible working is business as usual. Already seven out of 10 people work flexibly and nearly 10% are home-based. It has saved the company millions in terms of increased

---

[8] https://www2.bt.com/static/i/media/pdf/flex_working_wp_07.pdf

productivity and cut costs. It has also motivated our people and released more potential. At BT, we are attempting nothing less than the complete transformation of the way in which the company runs, the way we communicate, and the way we work together. We are eliminating as much bureaucracy and unnecessary control as possible."

At IBM[9], seventy per cent of employees now work from home at some part of the working week and three quarters of managers have remote employees. A huge investment has been made in training in acknowledgement of the complexities of managing a remote workforce effectively.

Alison Gregory, a senior managing consultant at the firm and who works part time said, 'Flexible working often means we need to work slightly differently in teams because we are a global business. For example, colleagues could take part in a conference call at 10pm because it's across different time zones but then trade this time for a later start the next day. It allows us to run global teams. It's about having the right people in the right place at the right time for the business. The only issue is to make sure that the person working flexibly is not working too hard. They need to adjust and if they aren't, managers need to challenge them about it.'

These examples are great and encouraging in that major employers are approaching the concept of work in different ways to allow greater flexibility for their people and that recognise the more global nature of the market. But much of this is about doing the same things more effectively and efficiently or sometimes just differently in order to create the impression of a modern working style.

This is not Guerrilla Working.

When Vodafone in New Zealand moved into a flash new building down at the Viaduct in Auckland they took the opportunity to completely rejig

---

[9] http://www.tutor2u.net/blog/index.php/business-studies/comments/ibm-powers-up-flexible-working-arrangements

their approach to 'in office' work, to consolidate several buildings and to optimise their return on the sizable investment in the new work space[10].

Their workforce was split into three groups: Homers; Zoners; and Roamers:

- Homers continued to have a dedicated desk space as the nature of their role and the tools, materials and resources they needed to perform their functions meant they were best staying in one place
- Zoners had a general space in the building/on a specific floor that meant they stayed with a team or business unit but didn't have a single dedicated desk
- Roamers were people who came into the office from time to time to 'touch down' or were otherwise generally free to work where ever they liked on any given day, including being on the road or working from home or satellite offices.

These changes certainly put the employees out of their comfort zones. There were teething troubles for the first couple of weeks and it definitely changed behaviours in the office. Some of the Zoners found that the change in work practices and lack of 'home space' took a while to get used to with many putting down roots at a Zoner desk, repeating their normal work patterns, only to be uprooted time and again.

Telecom New Zealand, not to be outdone by their competitors tried something similar at their subsidiary Gen-i[11]. They introduced 'hot-desking' amongst other initiatives. Most workers now arrive early in order to secure a desk for the day. Those who are unsuccessful in bagging a desk have to find vacant space to work from such as the lunchroom.

Such changes have little effect on changing core work behaviours

---

[10] https://www.vodafone.co.nz/a/pdfs/corporate-and-government/re-think-your-office-space-white-paper.pdf
[11] http://www.zdnet.com/is-hot-desking-so-called-because-its-hellish-1339320055/

because in general terms people are still working at a desk. It just happens to be in a slightly different place each day and it isn't as personal to them. What it has done, however, is to add an element of competition and probably stress to those workers each day. It's all a bit like musical chairs. Imagine for whatever reason someone is a bit late to work. They are going to be punished, unintentionally I am sure and forced to work out of their normal routine. Again this is putting the emphasis on work as a place and will encourage employees to be there in person rather than to be there in spirit.

Yahoo has recently reversed its approach and banned its staff from remote (predominantly home) working[12]. The change has been driven by the chief executive Marissa Mayer and recognises that 'Speed and quality are often sacrificed when we work from home'. The memo from Yahoo's human resources department banning employees from working from home said that 'Some of the best decisions and insights come from hallway and cafeteria discussions, meeting new people, and impromptu team meetings.' The reaction from many of the Yahoo workers was one of anger at the change and by many has been seen as a backward step.

Ideally having the opportunity to work with other people or in a different place should be seen as an opportunity to try something new. Guerrilla Working addresses such issues.

Mark Dorreen, Operations Director of the Light Metals Research Centre, part of Auckland Uniservice Ltd, the commercial arm of the University of Auckland, tells of a different environment however. 'We are pretty much an engineering consultancy, pushing into the technology space through the commercialisation of ideas developed through research into products. This is mostly in the global primary aluminium smelting market. As such we are working in aluminium smelters all over the world, with individuals or teams on site very frequently. So it has been the norm for us for a long time to be working remotely from home

---

[12] http://www.policymic.com/articles/28472/marissa-mayer-yahoo-remote-working-ban-a-smart-move-for-the-company

base.'

He adds that they 'have an established culture of very free communication to enable and support those who are away. From this we were confident enough to allow someone to shift back to their country of origin if that's what they want, and we are able to take on new staff in other countries, pretty much seamlessly, because for us it is just part of what normal looks like.'

Changes to the way that we work have to be brought about to bring benefits in terms of outputs that are of value to the employees and the customer or improve the productivity and performance of the organisation. Employees need to see the benefits to make these changes permanent. Guerrilla Working does this. It is about showing that truly flexible individual and group working is possible and sustainable.

But have we as humans changed? Are we really different creatures from the hunter gatherers that made up most of our evolutionary past?

Our lives are much more complicated yet our physical bodies have changed little in the last hundred thousand years. Sir Isaac Newton, working in the late seventeenth and early eighteenth century, is even today highly regarded as one of the most influential scientists of all time. He had a breadth of knowledge that was awe-inspiring. It still is. He was able to apply his mind to a wide range of subjects including mathematics, physics, mechanics and cosmology while still finding time to be the Warden and Master of the Royal Mint.

Today an individual would struggle with any one of these subjects. Scientists can spend their whole lives considering a tiny fraction of a subject. There is just too much knowledge and information available for one person to manage. The eruption in the amount of data is only going to exacerbate the issue.

Eddie Obeng describes this as the 'World after Midnight'[13] where our ability to understand and take in the world around us has been overtaken by the amount of knowledge out there. In Newton's day the key skill was to know and understand. Today's key skills are to be able to find and to interpret.

Perhaps tomorrow's skills will be to recognise patterns and read the stories the data are trying to tell us.

Obeng goes on to say that "Most of us spend our lives acting rationally in response to a world we recognise and understand but which no longer exists." This is true of our approach to the workplace. Our attitude to work is that it is still primarily a place that you go, somewhere that you have settled into and invested your own personal capital.

My own experience over many years of trying to move people from one building to another has shown that humans can understand the greater good and the macro level reasons why this is important but struggle to deal with it on a micro level. People struggle when changes in the workplace get personal.

The biggest issues that I have ever faced in such moves have been around the apparent minutiae such as where will I be able to make a cup of coffee, will my desk be left handed or right handed, what is parking like and can I walk to the shops in my lunch break? Ask anyone who has been through this process, especially when moving into a new building and they will tell you that their two biggest headaches are car parking and HVAC (heating, ventilation and air conditioning).

The issues of 'is this move right for the customer and right for the business' are way down on people's hierarchy of needs.

Work has changed and will continue to change. The second law of thermodynamics states that (forgive me for I paraphrase) 'In any closed system the amount of usable energy is always less than the total

---

[13] http://worldaftermidnight.com/

potential energy and as the amount of usable energy decreases entropy, the degree of disorder in the system will increase.'

This leads to two things. The first is that it does not matter how much energy you put into something, what comes out will be less than the effort you made. In other words it can take an awful lot of effort to achieve something fairly small. The second is that the natural order is for entropy to increase which means that there is a tendency for systems to move from a state of order to one of disorder. The very act of trying to maintaining things in a structured way, even just to keep them the way they were goes against the second law and demands a huge amount of effort and usable energy.

There is nothing certain in this world, apart from death and taxes but we can be absolutely confident that tomorrow will be different from today and that the workplace will become more and more complex.

So we need a new approach to work. Not one that is based upon physical structures but rather one that is based upon opportunity. Future organisations will need to respond much more quickly to rapidly changing customer demands and market conditions and to achieve this they need to think more about the effectiveness of their people rather than their physical assets or their hierarchical structures.

There is the quote attributed to Gaius Petronius Arbiter, the Roman Emperor Nero's adviser on elegance and good taste that goes along the lines of 'We trained hard, but it seemed that every time we were beginning to form up into teams we would be reorganised. … I was to learn later in life that we tend to meet any new situation by reorganising; and a wonderful method it can be for creating the illusion of progress while producing confusion, inefficiency and demoralisation.'

Apparently there is no written evidence of Petronius having said such a thing. The quotation first came to light at some time in the 1940s but everyone who ever reads it agrees and thinks that it describes the organisation that they happen to be working in.

So why is this so? If everyone knows that a reorganisation or a restructuring at work isn't going to make a real difference why do we keep doing it? Why do we fixate on the need for hierarchical structures?

Is it that there a basic need for humans to belong, to understand their place and role in society and that work is just an extension of this requirement? Do we need to know who the boss is and who our team mates are? This may have been fine when society was much less complex and being part of a tribe was essential for your own wellbeing and security but structures can get in the way of creating the kind of organisation that will address the issues that are being faced today and that most people want to work in.

Having rigid structures emphasised by organisation charts in neat blocks with straight lines (either continuous or dotted), leads to inter-team rivalries, confusion over priorities and the break down in essential communications. Defining teams in such hierarchies creates a loyalty to the team and an adherence to the will of its leader that is counterproductive to the overall aims and objectives of the organisation.

Teams are important and some degree of structure is essential but it must reflect the declared purpose of the business. It would make no sense at all to split a football team into separate forwards, mid-field and defensive teams with their own on field supervisors where all decisions need to go through the management structure to be agreed. So why does it make sense that we organise our work teams in such a way with separate customer, production, technical and administrative teams?

But sporting teams have different coaches to develop the different skills required to play in each position yet this adds to the argument. Sporting structures are arranged to create a single team approach with all players performing their different roles to complete a single objective which is to beat the opposing team. The role of management here is to develop the necessary skills and to get the team to work as a single unit.

Should this not be the same in business with organisational structures in place to improve decision making rather than to segment it and isolate authority into an elite meritocracy?

If the role of management is to make decisions however then the number of managers should be determined by the number of decisions that need to be made. More decisions should equal more managers. The number of decisions required is not something that is normally recorded in a management role yet the logical conclusion to this approach would be to have one decision maker and everyone else reporting to them. This doesn't happen.

Instead the number of managers is usually determined by the number of people in the organisation. More people leads to more managers and so their role must be people based, that is to create the environment in which the workers and the organisation flourish.

Following Local Government Review, where the two tier systems of local government was reduced to a single tier, the ICT Services of Durham County Council was split across four main sites and six smaller satellite sites. Each of the eight former district and county councils had had their own data centre and civic centre. A separate culture had grown up in each of the different buildings which were repeatedly reinforced by their isolation from the other centres and the management structures that existed.

There was a continuous pressure to collapse the number of buildings into one site for the whole of the ICT Services but this was at odds with the Council's stated desire to maintain a physical and visible presence within each of the sixteen main towns in the county. As long as there were customers spread around the county then an element of the ICT Services would need to be dispersed. Another way was needed to create the necessary culture to meet the changing needs of the authority.

Future organisations will need to be structured in ways that encourage people to share their knowledge, to work together to break down misunderstanding and improve the flow of work across the whole of the business. The concept of working for a boss and doing what they say will become outdated. Instead the focus will be on working to achieve a set of objectives or outcomes that marry the needs of the business with those of its customers. Steven R Covey describes this as a win win situation in his widely read book 'The 7 Habits of Highly Effective People'.[14]

Highly effective organisations will base their business model around identifying the needs of their market and will bring teams of people together to solve issues or realise opportunities that flow from this understanding. Structures will be ephemeral. People will be brought together for short periods and as the demands of the work change then so will the shape and structure of the teams responding to the challenges. Teams will become more project based and could include lay people, customers and industry experts.

It will be the interaction of the organisation's whole community of interest that will differentiate the successful businesses of the future and all of this will have very little to do with the building in which they operate or the organisational structure that is imposed upon them.

Work needs to be done where the customer requires it. If it needs to be face to face then there will be no substitute for direct human interaction. If it can be done more remotely then it will be the demographics of the customer or the type of product or perhaps the available infrastructure that will determine the best and most appropriate trading methods.

A lot of transactional work can now be done far away from the point of contact and without apparent reference to the customer. A recent experience of mine in buying an Insinkerator, an under the sink waste

---

[14] https://www.stephencovey.com/7habits/7habits.php

disposal unit highlights the point.

Having checked out the options available in the internet, the one I liked best was from a firm called www.sinks-taps.com, an organisation clearly devoted to all thinks sink related. I added my choice to the basket, registered as a new customer and hit the buy-now button. I put in my credit card details as requested and placed my order. The next day I received an email thanking me for my purchase and advising me that they would keep me updated with its progress.

Sure enough, a day later they let me know that the goods were on their way followed by a text (I'd given them my mobile number) saying when it would be delivered. The text gave me the option to change delivery to a more convenient date if the proposed date wasn't so. My new Insinkerator Model 45 arrived on time in a blue box and delivered by hand.

And this is what struck me. The whole process from selection to delivery had been smooth, efficient and effective but the first and only contact with a human that I was aware of was when the doorbell rang and the man in the brown and neatly creased overalls handed me the package. Even the signature transferring ownership was done electronically.

This will be an all too familiar tale for anyone who now buys off the internet but makes it very difficult for any organisation to differentiate their brand promise form their rivals other than through price.

Work is changing. The future will be different from today and the new approach starts with Guerrilla Working – the deliberate mixing up of people and teams, bringing talent together wherever it matters to solve issues and create opportunities. Groups of people come together drawing on their own experiences, developing new levels of understanding through different perceptions, building relationships and laying down new knowledge that can be used in addressing future challenges.

Guerrilla Working is a challenge to all of the procedures, practices and tenets that hold current organisations together but are in fact holding them back. It is not anti-management, opposed to structures or designed to do away with buildings. Instead it helps organisations to make the best use of the enormous talent that is locked upon inside their employees, their customers and other stakeholders.

Guerrilla Working enables the separation of the management of people and the delivery of task. It is not concerned with seeking permission or being concerned about standing on others toes, who is senior to who or whether or not it is their job to get involved. It allows managers to focus on working to develop the skills of their colleagues while ensuring that they broaden their experience and have the opportunity to work on what they most enjoy and therefore are most likely to be good at. It enables everyone to play their part in leading the organisation.

Hierarchy and structure is not an impediment as teams come together based upon experience, talent and a willingness to get involved. People from all parts of the organisation can come together purely because they believe that they have something to offer whether it be a direct understanding of the issue, having seen something like it before in a previous life or just a passing interest.

Dr Edward de Bono in his CoRT[15] Thinking courses (CoRT 4, Lesson 33) suggests the use of a random word to help break out of the way that we have always thought about things. He adds that: 'Escaping from the judgement system is difficult just as escaping from a reliance on critical thinking is difficult. We tend to return to what we know, our 'majority experience'. As a result, when dealing with new idea, we often think in a circular way, being 'stuck' with the same idea.

We need a new way to break from that 'circle', a new stimulus that will show us another 'path'. Doing that means using a technique that is random, unconnected to our experiences and inevitably, judgement.

---

[15] http://www.cortthinking.com/

The random input technique involves the introduction of something that is completely 'outside' the prevailing situation.' De Bono's suggestion for breaking out of a judgement system is the introduction of the word 'po'. A "po" is an idea which moves thinking forward to a new place from where new ideas or solutions may be found.

With Guerrilla Working the introduction of alternative or loosely related talent into the team acts in the same way. Fresh perception encourages the team to stop and think about its assumptions. A fresh pair of eyes can see the flaws in its customs and practices. An enthusiastic amateur can prove to be of much greater value than a disinterested professional.

A new manager can have a dramatic effect on a football team. Even their first match in charge can seem to be a complete turnaround in the fortunes of the club. It is next to impossible that they could have had enough time to implement any changes in tactics but their very presence has created the impetus to do something different. The players will make that extra effort to impress the new boss. They will feel more confident that the future is going to be rosier after all the person who was holding them back, who was to blame for their bad form has gone. And their opponents will not be feeling as confident as they were when the team had their old manager.

Guerrilla Working is not anti-building it just is not centred on them. The most important factors in creating teams that deliver are the dynamics within the people and the opportunity to come together to express and develop their thoughts and ideas. Having the right building helps but is not the determiner of good ideas and good solutions. This approach allows an organisation to make the most of all of the assets at its disposal including the physical and human irrespective of whether they have direct control over them.

Like a lot of good stories I am not sure how true this is but Joseph (Iosif Vissarionovich) Stalin, the Premier of the Soviet Union from 1924 until 1953, is reported to have said that if you want to know who really has the power you should watch who travels to who. The sentiment is that the weaker leaders will have to travel to visit the stronger ones who will be at an advantage by being on their own turf.

I'm not one to argue with Stalin, he could argue that he had a successful career, but Guerrilla Working turns this concept on its head in that the strongest leaders and workers will travel to the areas of the business that are most important and present the greatest opportunity for change. Stalin's approach was about playing mind games, taking a psychological approach to put his competitors at a disadvantage. He clearly saw negotiations as an opportunity to win at the expense of his opposition. This is not the win win that Covey describes and is not the outcome aimed for by using Guerrilla Working tactics.

That is enough history for now. This book is not about how to transform the work that you do or the workspace in which you find yourself. That is going to happen anyway. Instead this book is about how you can transform yourself and the people you work with to bring a different perspective and energy to what you do.

GuerrillaWorking is how small groups of people can come together to challenge the rules and achieve positive things in a short space of time. It is about passion, speed and low cost. It creates something special out of the ordinary, something daring, exciting and fun.

Guerrilla Working can become a reality by mixing up the people, involving the best of all of the talents to get stuck in and get back out again before everyone becomes too bogged down.

Blog entry: Low cost accommodation

I've been agile working for a long time when I come to think about it, really ever since the technology allowed from the early 90s but I had never got around to putting down my thoughts about it. That is until I started my blog and wrote this piece in a McDonald's restaurant somewhere in South East Northumberland:

How much does it cost to have high availability touchdown office space? 99p an hour that's how much.

If your work requires you to be about and about, if you are always on the move then having access to somewhere where you can connect to your systems in a secure way, to make use of that spare hour that you have between appointments can make the difference between being on top or chasing your tail. But don't worry, office space is available in every sizable town. Just grab your laptop or tablet and head for the golden arches. They are called McDonalds*. There are over twelve hundred in the UK and so you should never be that far away from one.

99 pence buys you a cup of tea and while you drink it you can make use of the free Wi-Fi. By using a secure Virtual Private Network client with dual factor authentication in a minute or so you are up and running with a desk and a comfortable seat. There are even toilets and of course refreshments. The only thing that you will lack for is electricity. I have never tested this however but have assumed that plugging your device

into a wall socket would be frowned upon and so make sure that your battery is well charged. (By the way, if you are really smart and use the loyalty card attached to the side of the cup you can get a free seventh cup for the price of six, reducing the cost to 85p per hour.)

OK so there are some downsides. People keep coming in and out, ordering food, the smell of which can drive you crazy. Kids play in the area set aside for them and make a lot of noise which competes with the musak that is a constant background and then there is the mild feeling of guilt that you are doing something which isn't quite right or fair. I'm not suggesting that this represents a serious alternative to ease your accommodation problems but for short drop down periods, allowing you to catch up and keep up to date it is definitely a viable option.

So here I am, looking out on the car park and sipping on my cup of tea. My email is up to date and I'm working on all of the documents that I need. I'm also working, if that is what it could be called, writing this blog. How agile is that?

*Other restaurants are available.

Why bother Guerrilla Working?

GuerrillaWorking is about involving the best of all of the talents, to challenge the rules and achieve positive things in a short space of time. It is about passion, speed and low cost. It creates something special out of the ordinary, something daring, exciting and fun.

This approach has many benefits and I will refer back to these throughout the book but these are some of the more obvious ones:

Uncover talent

Most organisations are full of talent yet much of it goes unnoticed. In truth we only take a part of ourselves to work. All of us are sons or daughters. Many of us will be brothers or sisters, parents or even grandparents. Among our immediate cohorts there will be wealth of untapped experience. Our colleagues will be chairing clubs, running charity drives, dealing with difficult family issues, balancing budgets, engaging in fascinating hobbies all while they are managing to hold down a job. Imagine if we could tap into this rich vein of experience. How much of it could be applied to the issues that we are facing and how much of the talent do we really realise of the person who sits next to us?

Shell is one of the world's largest multinational organizations with a global workforce of over 101,000 spread over more than 90 countries and territories. Their employees come from diverse cultural backgrounds and speak a multitude of languages. The company has developed its own intranet[16] that empowers employees to disseminate and contribute information, and communicate quickly and easily. Workers can take control of content, increasing accountability and ownership.

With as many as 3700 content authors updating at any one time, the intranet has created a culture of knowledge and information sharing throughout the business, leading to better, more-informed decision making worldwide. One of the key features of their intranet is that all employees need to list their skills and experience in their own biography page. On the back of this if a new project is set up requiring a specific set of skills then a simple search of the intranet highlights a short list of candidates for the job.

A similar intranet was set up by the students within the University of Arts London to advertise the projects that they were working on and to encourage people to get involved. For example of a student had an idea for a film but didn't have the experience they would ask for artist who had camera skills or acting skills to come forward, for free of course, and help make the film.

Guerrilla Working allows people to meet new people. It allows people to meet people they already know but in new ways. It allows them to build relationships in the most human of ways through face to face contact. Mixing people up in unusual contexts and situations will release unseen talents that can be combined to create a sum much larger than its parts. People will be able to tap into their life experiences and apply them to the work situations.

For example how useful would it be for a graphic designer to look at

---

16

http://www.intranetdashboard.com/press/case_studies/case_study_shell.pdf

designing processes? In business process engineering we look at defining the key task in a process and joining them up in a critical path but what would happen if we started with 'how can we make this process look beautiful?' Rather than using their skills to make things look attractive, could they be used to make things work attractive?

How useful would it be to ask the press office to write the release notes for the next software upgrade? Their talent is in getting stories out which have impact and that get the important points across very early in the copy. How many software developers could boast the same degree of talent?

How useful would it be to ask one of the team who is involved with charity work to help with a funding strategy? They will know hundreds of organisations that can be relied upon for funding. They will have a vast experience in writing successful bids that meet the criteria of an awarding body.

Visibility

Two of the biggest moans that I ever hear in any organisation are 'You never see management' and 'I don't know who is responsible for what.' Guerrilla working addresses both of these complaints head on. A management team that can be seen regularly working in and amongst its colleagues breaks down barriers and improves communications and understanding. It is always easier to make relationships with people in good times rather than when there is an issue between them. Having managers working alongside their teams in collaboration or just getting on with their work reduced suspicion in that there is an 'us and them' or that management is secretive and has something to hide.

When North Tyneside Council moved into a new administrative office on the Cobalt Business Park, Andrew Kerr, the chief executive at the time made a habit of having his lunch in the onsite Kaleidoscope restaurant whenever he could. Rather than sitting by himself or with his senior management team he would make the point of inviting himself to sit with other groups of employees. In this way he was able to break down barriers, learn important things about the business that he would otherwise not have heard and become highly visible. Occasionally he would meet his wife and daughter as well opening him up as a human being after all.

Taiichi Ohno, the father of the Toyota Production System (TPS) developed many methods to improve production as Toyota struggled to survive. Kaizen, the core technique of TPS, requires workers to observe carefully to see the facts of a situation and then to make maximum use of everyone's brainpower to devise simple, ingenious solutions to problems. Ohno coached his budding TPS leaders by drawing a chalk circle on the floor, telling them to stand in it for several hours observing reality, mind wiped clean, undistracted by things seemingly more important to do.[17]

While this kind of intensive observation is not always practical, having someone stand inside a chalk circle for hours may raise more questions than it answers, there is no substitution for in-the-raw experience. Guerrilla Working allows work activities to take place where the action is, where value is created and not remotely in some conference rooms.

If you want to know what your customers think of the business go and work where your colleagues interact with them. If you want to know why inventory levels are growing go and work in the warehouse and if you want to know why it takes sixty days to get an invoice paid for a supplier then go and work in accounts payable.

When somebody says to me 'I don't know who does what' then my response is invariably 'well go and find out then.' Again Guerrilla Working can address this issue. Sitting and working in amongst a team will soon give you a clear idea of who does what, who leads in which area and who the movers and shakers are. And of course it also does

---

[17] http://www.ame.org/sites/default/files/target_articles/02-18-1-Ohnos_Method.pdf

the reverse by showing them who you are.

Agglomeration

Trading estates are a common phenomenon found at the edge of most towns in the United Kingdom. They are filled with sheds selling anything from food to fence posts and clothes to carpets. What may seem odd at first sight is that often companies providing the same products will locate close to each other. You would think that competition would mean that providers would be spread fairly evenly throughout the available market but this is not true.

Instead shops come together on the basis that consumers will travel to a location to find what they are after. If you are going to buy a carpet then you are more likely to travel to a location which has more than one carpet shop. Having choice encourages more consumers to arrive leading to greater innovation and competition which leads to more consumers.

This is a simple example of the economics of agglomeration, a term used to describe the benefits that firms obtain by locating near each other. Drawing in additional consumers however is only one of its effects. Significant reductions in the cost of production may arise as they have access to competing suppliers and specialised labour markets.

It is believed that the growth of cities is fuelled by their ability to exploit economies of agglomeration. The basic concept is that production is facilitated when there is a clustering of economic activity.

Agglomeration can also take place within an organisation. By clustering their economic activities, natural competition takes over creating new development strategies. These help to draw information and increase the flow of new and innovative ideas. Just as having different firms together increases economic activity having people with differing perspectives creates new opportunities for service and product development.

Guerrilla Working agglomerates talent.

New realities

Guerrilla Working can add a degree of chaos to an apparently stable system using existing issues or problems at 'strange attractors' that can create new patterns and new realities.

Organisations look for certainty through their structures, their buildings and their market position yet we live in a chaotic system. Any system which has more than two variables is chaotic and is impossible to predict any more accurately than with a degree of probability. Our world is chaotic but one of the features of such systems is that patterns will emerge.

Think of the sea with all of the rocks and islands and winds and weather. How chaotic is this? Yet the waves crash against the shore in almost parallel lines and with metronomic frequency. Think of the weather with all of its winds and rain and clouds and drought. The weather is another chaotic and unpredictable system yet clouds appear with similar shapes, storms are formed and whirlwinds appear. These are all regular patterns which emerge and these are not just earthly phenomena. Look at our universe with its billions and billions of variables yet the same patterns of stars, galaxies, planets and comets appear over and over again.

These patterns emerge around what in physics are described as strange attractors, a stable, non-periodic state or behaviour exhibited by some dynamic systems, especially turbulent ones that can be represented as a nonrepeating pattern in the system's phase space.

Mixing the workplace up by introducing new faces and challenging the status quo will have a dramatic effect on the creative output of an organisation. Like a cat among the pigeons, destabilisation may well create a new stability.

Provocation

I have already described De Bono's use of the word 'po' to help us break out of traditional ways of thinking and practices. In his book 'I Am Right You Are Wrong' he proposes that the human mind is a self-organising and a pattern making system.

In order for humans to be able to function the brain forms patterns and uses these to allow rapid decision making. As an example, once we know what a dinner plate looks like we are able to recognise it instantly from almost any angle. Without this patterning attribute decisions would take much longer than we can afford. The simple act of putting on eleven items of clothing has just fewer than forty million possible combinations yet we manage to do it every morning in a couple of minutes.

Close your eyes and think of a Lego brick, any brick. What colour is it? What size and shape is it? For me it is a red four by two, not a green one or a yellow one or a blue one, not a three by two, or a two by two or an eight by two. It isn't an odd colour like orange or white and it isn't an odd shape like a roof section or a base plate. It is a red four by two. Of all the bricks that I could have chosen this is the one that pops into my head when I hear the word Lego. What is it for you?

Of course I know about all of the other bricks. I've seen them on the television, I've seen them on the web and in the shops and I even have seen them on a trip to LEGOLAND. I know about the Star Wars products and the Harry Potter collection and I'm familiar with the Duplo and Technics ranges. I have bought Lego for my children and played with it many times, building towers, houses, cars and all sorts of other interesting things. I've also stood on some in my bare feet or knelt on a piece and have let out an expletive or two.

Every word we come across has an immediate association for us. We cannot help it as it is how our brain works by linking what we see and what we hear with an image or a thought, by forming patterns. It is an instant process and is how we avoid danger and how we spot an opportunity. It is a positive force that has helped us to evolve and lead to our undoubted success.

The word 'po' was inspired by other words such as hypothesis and provocation and is to be used to help our minds leap out of existing patterns and into possible alternatives. Being able to pattern is very useful as in the dinner plate example but can also restrict thinking in that anything that closely resembles a dinner plate will be seen as one in our mind's eye.

Guerrilla Working can and will act as a provocation allowing people to see things in a new light. It will encourage teams to break out of preconceived patterns of work, the way they have always been done around here and to reflect on possible alternatives.

You will have heard it said that necessity is the mother of all invention. Many inventions and changes come about during periods of crisis and high tension. A similar common expression is 'Cometh the hour, cometh the man.' Huge advances in technology take place during war for example. The development of a new radical product often leads to a myriad of follow on products. Think what you can do with a mobile phone today as opposed to a few years ago, especially with a smartphone. You can even use them to ring people.

These advances come about due to a change in paradigm. A single idea gives birth to thousands just as single genetic mutation can lead to new species. The process of coming up with new ideas is difficult to comprehend or formulate but specific acts of provocation or interventions can provide the mental leap from our existing patterned behaviour into new ones.

Add fun

What is the most exciting thing that you can ever do at work? For me it is the opportunity to get involved in something new, something that is challenging but is going to make a big difference to the business and its customers.

Frederick Herzberg[18], clinical psychologist and pioneer of 'job enrichment' and regarded as one of the great original thinkers in management and motivational theory acknowledged the complexity of salary as a motivator (money, earnings, etc.), and concluded that money is not a motivator in the way that achievement and recognition are. Everyone works for money but once they are used to their income its effect as a motivator wears off quickly.

Having worked in Information and Communications Technology for many years now I am aware that the most important motivator to the technically minded is to keep providing new experiences and things to learn. It has long been said that the way to reward good people is to give them more work. Keeping people busy and stretching them to the edge of their ability is often reward enough providing that their remuneration is reasonable. People rarely leave a job solely for more money but rather to look for a new challenge. By the way it is worth stating at this point that if you are very busy at work then you must be very good.

Guerrilla Working creates new opportunities for people to get involved in areas of a business that they may not be used to. They get to play with new toys, meet new people, bring different perceptions and rise to new challenges. This adds excitement to the business and is fun.

Guerrilla Working has two main aspects. The second is bringing together teams of like-minded individuals who want to make a difference and the first is the subject of the following chapter.

---

[18] http://www.businessballs.com/herzberg.htm

Blog entry: A great day at the office

Guerrilla Working isn't just about understanding process and looking for opportunity to bring talent together. It is also an effective way of binding people to the organisation in which they work:

Tuesday 30 July was a great day at the office. I started and finished the day with a couple of strategically important meetings and I felt like I was moving the business forward. In between I had some other meetings and talked to some very interesting people but these only made the day good.

But Tuesday was a great day. I didn't solve world peace or fed the poor. I didn't even do anything that you could say had made that much of a difference but I was able to do the thing that I most enjoy. I met and talked to people.

It happened because I was trying my Guerrilla Working. I was parked outside of the Cabinet Office, tapping away on my laptop and waiting for my first meeting when I remembered that I had lost my door entry card. It also allows me to use the fantastic new Multi-Functional Device printers so losing it was quite a blow. Anyway, who should walk by but the woman whose job it is to issue new and replacement cards. I'm sure she does other things as well but we got talking and she agreed to help me with a re-issue. Xiaoling is her name by the way and we had a bit of a laugh and a joke while the card printer did its stuff. The funny thing was I was wearing the same suit and tie as when I had the original photo taken.

David the caretaker passed by and we said hi. I hadn't seen for some time and he came over and we chatted for a while about how things were going. Well it would seem.

Armed with my new card (thanks to my NBF Xiaoling) and out of my first meeting I needed to print some papers and so headed off to the nearest printer. I can use anyone, anywhere in the county and I got chatting to the person already printing off some stuff. We talked about how good the new devices were, at least I said that and she agreed and we had a bit if a laugh and a joke. Suzanne was her name, the printer told me that and I remembered it for the next time I bumped into her.

So that was how my great day started, by meeting, engaging with and talking to people who play a role in running the organisation, just like me. Feeling a part of something is an important factor in anyone's work and I hope that the few minutes we spent together brightened their day, even just a little bit. It did mine.

Start with yourself

Even the longest journey starts with a single step and so having decided that it is about time that your organisation became more flexible in its approach you will need to start somewhere. You have three choices. You can either moan and whinge about how nobody understands the benefits that a new approach would bring and hope someone will latch onto it as an idea; you can put a project team together to build a business case that you take through senior management to get some traction; or you could go Guerrilla and try and do something about it yourself.

To start something new an organisation needs lone voices. Someone has to raise their head above the parapet and make a noise about what needs to change. You have bought the book and so you are clearly interested in the subject yet the only person that you can truly influence is yourself. If you want things to change in the organisation to which you belong then the best place to start is with you.

Working in an organisation which operates out of many buildings has its disadvantages. It means that you have to travel when face to face is required. It can also mean that both you and your colleague need to travel in order to get to the same place at the same time. This results in the inevitable periods when either you or your colleague are late.

If you are a Guerrilla Worker being early is no problem. You can simply sit at an empty desk, there is always at least one, open your laptop and get on with it. This what happened to me when I went to meet one of my internal customers whose office was a ten minute walk from where I was that day.

I arrived a little early to find he was held up with his last appointment and was indeed in another building. The receptionist asked if I would like to wait in his office but instead I asked if I could sit at one of the empty desks. Her eyebrows rose at my unusual request but she was happy to indulge me.

No sooner had I logged in when I heard someone say 'this computer is rubbish' (or words to that effect). As head of ICT Services it was difficult for me to ignore such a comment and for a few seconds I grappled with my internal daemons as to whether or not I should go and speak to them. Doing the right thing won and I got up, went over, introduced myself and asked what the matter was.

What followed was a useful conversation with lots of questions about the state of their technology, how soon it would be replaced and their preference for laptops over fixed desktops. All of these I was able to respond to and raised them with their manager when he finally arrived.

This is exactly what Guerrilla Working is about, experiencing and responding to issues and opportunities as they happen on the ground. A previous chief executive once said to me 'He's the kind of person that would step over rubbish' and every time I'm faced with the choice to ignore something or address it his words ring in my ears. I could have chosen to ignore the comment, pretend that I hadn't heard it after all it wasn't aimed at me personally yet that is not the person I want to be. I started with myself.

I heard some time later that after I'd left the person who had made the original comment asked 'Was that really the Head of ICT?' Such engagement is clearly not a usual experience for them.

Before you can think about getting groups of Guerrilla Workers together you are going to have to set to work on yourself. This will require you to address aspects of the way that you work both in the physical and in the psychological

So, sit back in your chair, relax and ask yourself, 'Am I truly ready to become a Guerrilla Worker?'

Could you get up now and start to work somewhere else perhaps in the same building, in another building, at home or on the beach? Are you really flexible or are you still wedded to the four walls of your office. Could you cope without the life support systems at your disposal? Do you have the brass neck to march into another office and get started?

The answer is probably no, at least not yet and so a plan is needed.

To be a Guerrilla Worker you are going to have to change the habits of a working lifetime and it is going to feel strange at first. It will be a constant battle between your desire to be true to the cause and the comfortable sensations you feel when you slip your feet underneath your old desk.

Let's start with the physical. The plan needs to result in you having all of the things that you need to do your job at your disposal and in a way that they can be taken with you wherever you happen to be.

Define your job

Before you decide what you need to do your job you need to define what your job is. You will have a number of sources for this information such as a job description, although this will list things you probably don't do, or your curriculum vitae. The best source however is probably what is in your head. Try looking through your calendar and jot down all of the different types of activities that you have been involved in and this should give you a clue.

Earlier in my management career I found myself sifting through piles and piles of ruled computer printout paper. I was working for Spicers[19] in the office products market as a depot General Manager. Sales were important as was the quality of the picking and distribution operation and so there were lots of numbers that had to be looked at as well as a significant amount of correspondence with customer and suppliers. I would spend most of my available office time between sales calls sorting through the paper and doing what I thought was important. I was becoming increasingly irritated however by the interruptions from my team. No sooner had I got my head around a report than someone would stick their head round the door and ask a question. It was a constant stream and I was annoyed because they were getting in the way of my job.

It was then that I realised that it was the other way round. They were my job and the truth was that it was the paperwork that was getting in the way. Since then it has been unnecessary bureaucracy that has vexed me and I have made continuous efforts to try and minimise its disruptive effect. My real job was to be working with my team or out talking with customers. This was my first step to becoming a Guerrilla Worker.

So when you are defining what you do make sure it is what you should be doing rather than what you are doing. The two can be quite different.

A friend of mine who works in the Police told me how a very experienced colleague was retiring. His Chief Constable was concerned because the kind of policing he got involved in was not on his job description and he was going to be difficult to replace.

The genius of the Chief Constable however was that he had the unusual but obvious perception that the best person to describe a role is the person who is currently doing it. So he asked him to write down what he did. The genius of the soon to be retired policeman however was

---

[19] http://www.spicers.co.uk/

that he had a ready-made methodology to provide what the Chief Constable required.

On a piece of paper he wrote down four sets of five things that the replacement would need and handed it to his boss. I have added some examples in parenthesis which may be of help if you wish to follow the example.

- What five things did he need to know to do the job? (A list of customers, product margins, pricing policies)
- Which five systems or processes were key to doing the job? (Payroll, financial system, production control etc.)
- Which five key people did he interact with in order to fulfil his role? (Betty who can arrange appointments, Tony who knows everyone, Bill who pulls all of the strings etc.)
- What five things did he wish he had been told before starting the job? (What the aims of the organisation are, how governance works, who has the best coffee etc.)

Try it.

What things do you need?

Now that you have identified the job role that you are trying to fill, the next stage is to decide what you need to have to hand in order to be able to carry out that function.

Imagine it's the back end of November, Christmas is just around the corner and it is cold. It's lashing down with rain and it's a perfect day for the boiler to break down. You have no hot water and no central heating and the house feels like a fridge in a few minutes. You ring for a plumber who turns up at your door. What would you expect them to be wearing? Overalls perhaps that offer protection against some of the hazardous chemicals that they may use, with lots of pockets to keep their tools in. What would you expect them to bring with them? Hopefully they will be carrying a tool box with a blow torch, some spanners, some copper piping, various fittings and a meter to test the gas.

What would you think if the plumber arrived at your door wearing a bowler hat and carrying a briefcase? Not very impressed I would imagine. So what is it that your customers would expect you to turn up wearing and carrying?

Paul Tanney told me, when he was Chief Executive of East Durham Homes, a Registered Social Landlord responsible for thousands of social tenants, that you should dress as your customers would expect you to. His wise words have stuck with me and I have thought about them many times when going to a conference or a public event. I'll leave what you wear up to you however. You should know your customers better than I do.

What are the essential things that you need to perform your role? Look around at your desk and your office. Think about all of the things that you have around you and whether or not they are essential for you to take with you. To be a Guerrilla Worker you will have these things with you at all times. You'll need to travel light and so weight and size are going to be an issue.

If you are like most people who work in an office you will have a desk covered in paper, stationery, photographs of loved ones and other paraphernalia that mark it out as your territory. There will be draws in the desk filled with files, more stationery, unread reports and keepsakes. You will have some shelves with books, printed reports, more photographs and perhaps some awards. The list will go on. Your office life will have filled credenzas, cupboards, filing cabinets, table tops and no doubt a couple of storage boxes that you have been meaning to clear out for years. The amount of stuff you have can be a correlation of the amount of time you have been there. Detritus will have accumulated over the years like sediment at the bottom of the sea.

What goes for your office may well be the same in your home. Snappy

Living suggests using the Six Month Rule[20] suggesting that you make a commitment to get rid of anything you haven't used in the past six months (aside from seasonal items designed only to be used once a year). Generally speaking, if you haven't used something in six months, you're almost surely never going to use it.

Now, of course, there are exceptions. When you are tackling your office they will pop into your head and you should try to ignore them.

- It could come in handy. Sure it could – for someone. But if you haven't used it in the last six months, maybe that someone isn't you.
- It cost a lot. It's painful to get rid of stuff you once paid dearly for. It means you wasted money or got taken in by a gimmick. But keeping the item isn't going to turn a bad buy into a good one. It just means this mistake you made (and we all make them) is owning you longer than it should. Learn from it and move on.
- They don't make it anymore. And if you haven't used it in six months, maybe now you know why it's no longer being made.
- It's associated with something sentimental. But how important is the sentimentality of an item you haven't thought of in months, or probably years? You only have room in your life for so many mementos. There's a big difference between keeping an artlessly carved seagull that your child made and keeping one you bought from a souvenir stand on a beach.

If you think you've found an exceptional item – one you need to keep even though you haven't used it in months – ask yourself a few questions:

- Can you think of three uses for it?
- If it's a single use type item, can you think of something you want to do with it this week?
- Why did you not use it in the past six months, if it's so useful?

---

[20] http://snappyliving.com/if-you-havent-used-it-in-the-last-six-months-get-rid-of-it/

Of course there are some things that you will have to keep, some by law and others because they are important but I will come back to these later in the chapter.

Clearly there are some things that you can carry and there are some things that you cannot. A desk for example would be difficult but how much of a problem is this? Take a walk along the corridor or have a look around if you work in an open plan office and count how many empty desks there are. Most offices even when they are full will have an occupancy rate of around 75 per cent. Some people will be on holiday or off sick and this will account for about 15 per cent of the total workforce. The rest will be covered by people who are in meetings, out visiting customers are working at another site. Finding a spare desk, and chair, is usually not a problem. White boards and flip charts are also usually available as well.

In truth as an office based worker there is probably very little that you need to carry to do your job. Modern technology helps and I will address this in a later chapter but your core needs will be well served using communications tools.

I drag all the stuff that I need behind me in a flight bag with zipped pockets, wheels to make it easier to move and a long handle to pull it along with. (The caretakers always ask me where R2D2 is if I am ever without it.)

Inside the main pocket I keep my laptop and its charger along with my phone charger. I used to have a day book that I wrote in occasionally and any paperwork that I hadn't sorted including printed reports that I want to read but I no longer carry them. All documents are filed on my laptop or available through the central servers. Only if I'm going far will I also carry a book for something to read.

In the front pocket I used to have spare ink (I used a fountain pen in the mistaken belief that it makes me write better), a biro, a pencil, some highlighters, some dry board markers and a pair of scissors. Earlier in the year I stopped carrying any pens or pencils. I also have a spare pair of glasses, some tissues, some paracetamol and a retractable umbrella just in case and that is it.

Apart from the phone in my pocket, this is all that I need to discharge my duties. As long as I have my bag with me I can settle down anywhere and work. If I am within the network I can access all the documents I need. If I am away from the organisation's buildings then as long as I am able to get a wireless connection then I am able to log in securely and again access everything I need. It is amazing how many cafes and restaurants offer free wireless access to the internet and so for the price of a cup of tea I am able to do work on my laptop as normal. If I can't get wireless then I can connect using my smartphone or make use of its applications.

It has taken me many years to whittle the contents of my bag to its latest minimalist iteration. I used to carry much more including a network cable, flip-chart markers and a stapler. I wore out the wheel bearings of a few flight bags before getting the message.

I haven't managed to work out an effective way of having a cup of coffee without resorting to buying one however.

This is my list though and it suits the job that I do. Only you can decide what is right for you role but the aim of Guerrilla Working is to maximise the time that you can spend communicating with your customers and your team by being in amongst them.

Dealing with paper

As Michael Scott, played by Steve Carell, said in the US series of the Office 'Real work is done on paper, now type that into your laptops.' Learning to do away with paper is going to be the biggest issue that you are likely to face in going Guerrilla. Most organisations are addicted to it. Remember the promise of the paperless office?

Walking past the office of a colleague of mine one day I noticed that his desk was empty and not its usual black diamond ski run of paperwork. I jokingly asked his PA 'What's wrong with John's desk?'

'What do you mean?' she replied.

'Well it's normally covered with paper and it's now completely clear.'

'Oh that,' she laughed 'he's gone on holiday.'

On the floor of his office was a black bin bag filled with the papers that had presumably been the covering for his desk until yesterday. If he was able to throw them away now why did he feel the need to keep it all in the first place?

Paper will keep coming at you and how you deal with it will need to be part of your support system. I will cover this later. Most of it will be periodicals and marketing material but there will also be documents to authorise and invoices to pay. There are also the printed copies of reports and memos that you will have already received electronically, sent to you just in case by those who are someway behind your thinking.

Paper is heavy stuff and is not something that you will want to lug a lot of around with you. It needs to be dealt with straight away if possible. Is it a document that you will likely read? If no then throw it out immediately. Is it available electronically? If yes then do likewise. If you don't need it then you don't need it. If you are not sure then you don't need it. The only paperwork that you should end up carrying are those that still need a physical signature or for some reason are not available in an electronic format. If you can, find a way to change the system so that you don't need these either.

A friend of mine who worked in Paris and hopped on planes between there and the UK a lot became so obsessed with the weight of what he was carrying that after he had read a page in a paperback he would tear it out of the book and throw it away. A bit extreme perhaps but it certainly makes a point.

Brown Brothers used to be an independent distributer of parts and paint to the automotive aftermarket until it got swallowed up by Unipart. When I was in charge of their Edinburgh depot I recall having a conversation with the Regional Sales Manager for Scotland and North East England. He carried everything he could with him. Admittedly these were the days before mobile computing but he had sales figures going back years.

'I have all the information to hand that I need' he said, 'I can find the sales of any line for the last five years.'

'That's interesting' I genuinely added.

'Yes' he carried on, 'I can make comparisons of sales and margin month on month. I can spot and analyse trends.'

'I'm afraid that I don't have any of that with me.' I responded with feigned apology.

'So what do you do if you need to know how sales are going compared to a couple of years back?' he asked.

I smiled. 'I ring you.'

Even if you throw something out that would have actually been quite useful don't worry. Paper maybe cumbersome but its beauty is that someone else always keeps a copy.

I have managed to go paperless now. I've been agile for some time and am obsessed with being more personally efficient yet I still hung onto some of the vestiges of the old way of doing things.

I still read books and magazines and I might write my shopping list occasionally on a scrap of paper when at home but at work I am all electronic. If anyone should lead the way in being paperless then it should be the Head of ICT Services.

This is what I have done. I have set up a 'Today' folder in Explorer and within that I have set up a folder for each day for the rest of the week. I put all documents for meetings into each folder and I've created a word document for each day which will act like my day-book. I've also set up a 'To Do' task.

When I am in a meeting I keep notes on my daily word document and annotate any of the reports if appropriate. I then transfer actions to my 'To Do' list, send notes to those who should see them and then discard the stuff I have not used. At the end of the day I file everything where it should go. I set these all up on a weekly basis as part of my end of week preparations.

The day-book is no more.

Support systems

There is that corny and endearing but unlikely story that President Kennedy was visiting NASA one day when he met a janitor sweeping the floor. They got into a conversation and the president asked him what his job was to which the janitor replied 'I'm helping to put a man on the moon.'

The story is often used to describe how great leadership makes sure that everyone is involved in the vision of an organisation but for me it describes how no person can work in isolation. As John Donne wrote 'No man is an island, Entire of itself, Every man is a piece of the continent, A part of the main.'

When Neil Armstrong stepped out of the Apollo 11 Lunar Module he was the tip of a very large iceberg. Thousands of people had worked together over many years to enable him and Buzz Aldrin to spend a few hours on the moon's surface. I am sure that there were janitors in the team.

Becoming a Guerrilla Worker may not be as glamorous or cutting edge as flying to the moon and back but never the less it will help you enormously if you have some sort of ground crew to help you with your mission. If you can access a resource to scan documents, make appointments, filter sales calls and the like it will free up more of your time to be doing what you have set out to do. I've worked with a PA close by, with a PA three hundred miles from where I was based and without a PA at all. Having one is not essential but my experience is that it is of great benefit to have someone who truly understands what it is that you are trying to achieve and is working to support you. To make this happen you need to build a very close relationship with your ground crew.

It also helps if you can build a team of people around you who are someway along the same road as you.

Keeping a base camp

When I first worked for Durham County Council I was nominally based at the Rivergreen Centre which was a few hundred metres away from County Hall. The accommodation there was much better and ultra-modern, when compared to the main civic building, as it had been built as a possible location for the North East Assembly but which never got off the ground. It suited me well to work there as I was close enough to the action but far enough away to have a degree of autonomy.

Shortly after I joined I got a phone call to ask if the person on the other end could borrow my office in County Hall.

'But I don't have an office in County Hall' I said, 'I'm based up here in Rivergreen.'

'Yes you have,' came the reply 'it's up on the fifth floor and it's got your name on the door.'

Armed with this information I hot-footed it down through the woods to County Hall, climbed the five flights of stairs and there it was, room 5/109. My name was on the door and there was a desk and a conference table but little else. I didn't need an office but I discussed it with the rest of my management team and we all felt that it was too good a resource to let go. Having somewhere to meet right at the heart of the operation would prove to be very useful.

The only problem was that it looked unoccupied and so unwanted. A quick trip to a local retailer and I had a vase and some photo frames to make the office looked lived in.

Room 5/109 has its own calendar now and you can book it by inviting it to a meeting to which it will reply yes or no if it is available. It has proved its worth as a valuable resource as a meeting room but also as a base to come back to and regroup from time to time. I have to make sure its empty and get kicked out when there is something more important pressing.

Guerrilla Working is about breaking the link between where you work and what you do. This doesn't mean that you should have no office or desk that you could claim to be your own. It is about putting this into perspective to ensure that your personal space doesn't become what you do or who you are and doesn't present a barrier between you and your colleagues.

Since I started writing this book I have broken all ties with what used to be my office. I have got rid of the desk and changed the name on the door to the 'Room for Improvement'. Most people don't notice at first but those who do, those who get lost when looking for the room, smile and chuckle and ask what it is all about and I tell them the story of how I was changing, how I had said to myself that the business needed to change and the only person that I could truly influence was myself.

It started as a statement, a joke perhaps but it is deadly serious. After all, the biggest room in any business should be the room for improvement. Is it where you work?

Your working career should not be defined by where you go but by what you achieve. It is the nature of today's labour market that jobs will come and go. In a recent study of two thousand British workers, 'Your Working Life Laid Bare'[21] the average person will have six jobs throughout their working lives and have ten interviews. In the United States the figure quoted for the number of jobs is between seven and eleven (10.5 actually but I'm not sure how you can have half a job) but these things are notoriously difficult to measure.

Now a man can drown in a pond that averages 10cm deep and so there must be some people who have many more jobs than six and this would appear to be an increasing trend. A job for life used to be the norm yet in many ways it still is. I could argue that I have been doing the same job, more or less, since I started, it is just that I have been doing it for different organisations and in different places and with different teams.

We must not become obsessed by location unless it is relevant to the customer or the business. Having an office is not in itself a bad thing but adherence to it as part of what you do is.

Maintaining a presence

So far this chapter has considered the physical changes that you will need to consider before becoming a Guerrilla Worker but there are also the psychological aspects as well. You will be stepping into some uncharted territory and so you need to prepare.

The word Guerrilla can seem to be exciting, daring and even fun. But it can also be menacing, after all it means little war.

The word was first used in the Napoleonic Wars during the Peninsular War (1807 -1814), which lasted until Napoleon was defeated in 1814. The word was first used in Britain as early as 1809 yet it is often considered as much more of a twentieth century phenomenon. The Peninsular War was regarded as amongst the first wars of national liberation and was significant for the emergence of the widespread use of guerrilla warfare.

The key elements of guerrilla warfare are the use of small and

---

[21] http://www.thisismoney.co.uk/news/article-2299486/Your-working-life-laid-bare-Six-jobs-12-pay-rises-125-days-sick--office-romance.html

manoeuvrable forces competing against larger and more traditional armed forces. Sound familiar? Guerrillas however rely very heavily upon the assistance of the local population to provide them with sustenance, local knowledge especially of the terrain and shelter.

One of the primary requirements for a successful guerrilla campaign is for it to have the support of the local populace which allows guerrilla fighters to blend back into the background easily. Che Guevara described his understanding of guerrilla warfare as being 'used by the side which is supported by a majority but which possesses a much smaller number of arms for use in defence against oppression.'

Just as a pack of wolves picks off the weaker and less protected members of a herd the guerrilla fighters look to take on peripheral targets or smaller groups of enemy troops which are easier to overcome, keeping their own losses to a minimum and causing the maximum amount of impact in the opposing troops. Rather than trying to wipe out the enemy the aim is to weaken it as a fighting unit forcing it to eventually abandon its aims and withdraw.

Chinese communist leader Mao Zedong described the basic tactics of guerrilla warfare as: 'The enemy advances, we retreat; the enemy camps, we harass; the enemy tires, we attack; the enemy retreats, we pursue.

So we need to remain mindful that the tactics and strategies that we are going to use as Guerrilla Workers may be a little daunting to the people we are going to work with. Anything new can be off putting and viewed with some suspicion. Our new found co-workers may view our actions as a possible threat and see us as potential spies in the camp and so we need to plan to overcome such fears.

This chapter is about preparing yourself rather than looking at others and I will return to how others may feel in the next chapter.

Let us consider though how you might feel as you become a Guerrilla Worker: shy; silly; harassed; unnerved; out of your depth;

unappreciated; on your own; all of the above perhaps.

Remember that the purpose of becoming a Guerrilla Worker is to uncover talent, increase visibility, create new realities, provoke ideas and to have fun. You are going to be spending a lot of time among unfamiliar faces, at first, and to be effective, you may need to become a different person than you are today, perhaps more visible, more approachable and more open.

When you are away in the field your colleagues will need to know where you are even more so than they do when you are office bound. No longer can they simply knock on the door of your office to find you. If you have an electronic calendar then opening it up is a good start. If you don't have one then it's time to get one.

An electronic calendar that is open to all employees is an excellent way of setting out your intention to be visible. People will be able to see where you are, who you are with and what you are doing. Should someone wish to meet with you then all they have to do is to look at your appointments and select a time when you are available. Truly private appointments, such as a visit to the hospital, can remain just that, truly private.

Being seen as available can be more important in perception than in reality. Tom Farmer, the founder of Kwik-Fit reportedly made the bold decision to publish his home phone number after a spate of customer complaints. Thankfully no one rang him either because the Kwik-Fit managers made sure that all complaints were dealt with quickly or that no customer thought the problem was big enough to worth ringing him. But no one could accuse Farmer of trying to hide from the issue.

As a Guerrilla Worker you are going to be seen in a lot of unusual places which means, by default that you won't be seen as often in the usual places. The trick will be to appear as if you are everywhere and a good social media presence will go a long way to creating such an impression.

This book is not the place to discuss the relative merits of the differing social media platforms but using the right tools can allow people to be aware of who you are, your values, your interests and what you are up to. You can even use it to show where you are.

Social media can increase your perceived presence to be much greater than you could spread yourself physically. It shows that you are not afraid to share your thoughts and engage.

My own favourite platform is Twitter which I use to disseminate interesting information relevant to what I am up to both at work and with my 'outside' interests, as well as letting people know where I am or will be. The discipline of only being able to use 140 characters means that messages have to be short and to the point, which can be quite a challenge. Twitter is also full of humour and normally has a relaxed feel and approach in keeping with a more open and visible management style.

I blog using Wordpress and anyone who wants to get a flavour of what makes me tick only has to put my details into a search engine. I will let the reader judge whether or not my blogs are worth the read but I feel that it is important for to be expressing myself in a way that is accessible. I also write a short blog each week at work for the same reason and publish it on the Council's intranet. These pieces are very much focussed on what is coming up in the next week or so and give some indication of why they are important. This blog doesn't replace other communications but rather reinforces them using an informal and more inclusive style.

Although social media appears relaxed it still requires a degree of discipline. Having made a commitment to have an online presence it needs to be maintained. Dipping in and out of it as and when you can be bothered is not going to create the impression of visibility and availability that is wanted and so time needs to be set aside to develop ideas and to post regular contributions.

Getting involved in other's social media helps as well. Re-tweeting, liking and commenting all add to your online presence, improve your visibility and show that you are willing to engage on the serious and the trivial. It breaks down the impression that distance and location matters.

Instant messaging is another great tool. I will raise the subject of Unified Comms in a later chapter but this allows you to engage in online conversations instantly. Having your status button green shows that you are available and out there somewhere working. If someone needs to get in touch then it is a very quick and obvious method of being able to do so.

Good old-fashioned email gets a bad press these days, principally on the back of its misuse yet it still remains a potent way of keeping in touch. There are many complaints about mail such as that there is just too much of it and that a lot of it is unwanted spam, that people email you when they are sat two desks away rather than coming across and talking to you and that it is used to copy in everyone in the world in order to cover their backs.

A quick response to an email though shows the writer that what they have sent you is important and that you have taken notice. After all, you have taken the time to read it and respond. Just as an unexpected text from a loved one can give you a warm glow then a response can create the impression that you care, because you do.

Email is just another form of communication. In itself it is not inherently good or bad. It is certainly not evil. Good communication requires a mix of tools, techniques and media. The over reliance upon one method will dilute its effectiveness and potentially alienate yourself from much of your audience. Some people who you are trying to engage with will only be interested in email whereas others will prefer face to face, or video or perhaps a more formal report. Only by spreading the methods that you use can you ensure that you get effective coverage of your intended audience and your messages out.

And that is the beauty of Guerrilla Working in that you can maximise face to face time with a wide audience while maintaining a good communications mix using the other tools and methods at your disposal. But this all takes effort, planning and constant vigilance to be certain that you are not missing out some important groups or individuals.

So now you have got yourself sorted and ready to go into action. The next step and the subject of the next chapter is to prepare your approach.

Blog entry: Doing a Phil

One of the first things I did when starting my current role was to give up my office. The service was based in various facilities around the county but I had been given space at a new building known as Rivergreen and a short walk from County Hall where most of my senior management colleagues were based. Being away from the headquarters has always suited me as I feel that I can have more influence over the culture of my team.

The room in which my desk was situated was the only meeting room that we had and was far too big for one person. The desk was cowering in one corner as if it was afraid to be there and in the middle of the room was a large conference table. I never like being locked away and much prefer to be out and about, in amongst the people and so it was an easy decision to make.

Management isn't about elitism and isolation, it is about engagement and understanding and so the management team made a collective decision that none of us would have offices, instead we would sit out in the general office. A separate array of desks was selected for the team, a pod as it was known at the time. Four desks were enough for the managers but there wasn't one from me. Instead I would sit wherever there was a space.

And there always is a space, an empty desk somewhere. No matter how fit and healthy your people are there are always some away on holiday (on average 16%) or at meetings somewhere else. I would take the opportunity of asking the person sitting next to a seemingly vacant plot if the desk was free, sit down and get on with it.

At first there was some reticence from my new-found neighbours. There was some suspicion that perhaps I was picking on them, choosing them as individuals to keep an eye on or that there was an ulterior motive for picking that spot. Like a fox among the rabbits there was unease until my intentions were made clear and some general chit chat soon broke down any immediate barriers. Some individuals are naturally engaging and are happy to have new people amongst them while others are more reluctant to strike up a conversation but that is not the point. I'd make the effort to try and sit at desks that I hadn't visited before, in amongst people that I didn't know as well.

Soon my work station wanderings became accepted as the norm or at least normal for me but I realised that I had made a breakthrough of sorts when I heard of one of the team leaders had been sitting working in amongst another team. His normal place of work was at Seaham but he had been in Durham for a meeting and had some spare time and so had found a vacant desk and got on with it. Apparently this had now become known as 'doing a Phil'.

Prepare your approach

George Bernard Shaw said that 'Reasonable people adapt themselves to the world. Unreasonable people attempt to adapt the world to themselves. All progress, therefore, depends on unreasonable people.

I don't agree. I want to be reasonable, have sound judgement and good sense but I want to change the world. I want to live in a world that is reasonable and Guerrilla Working is how I am going to make a difference.

Guerrilla Working is going to change your approach to work. You're going to start a revolution with repercussions that will be felt right across your organisation. You'll be hailed as a hero, the people's champion and in future they'll tell their grandchildren of the changes you instigated and the great things that were achieved on the back of them.

So where are you going to start? If you don't know where you are going then any road will do.

Everything starts with a vision. Is there some area of the business that you would be comfortable giving it a go in or is there somewhere that is crying out for change? Are you up for a challenge or would it be better to cut your teeth on something a little less daunting?

Perhaps before you answer these questions we should really consider what it is that you want to achieve. We have already covered that Guerrilla Working is going to help you address a number of issues (uncover talent; increase visibility; create new realities; provoke ideas; and to have fun) but most organisations are complicated and you will not be able to change everything or influence everyone at once.

Your efforts need to be focussed on whatever criteria you choose. It's your plan and so you can start with an area that shows the greatest opportunity, or perhaps the area that is of greatest interest or even an area that you think will offer the least resistance. Having a plan and a vision will help you to keep on track, it will remind you why you are doing this on the days where things don't go as well as you had expected.

Start with the obvious, inside your organisation or outside? If this is a new experience then you are probably on safer ground to start somewhere within your own business. You will already know most of the ropes. Your new found colleagues may be intrigued as to why you are sitting working next to them but they hopefully won't challenge your right to be there. You should be in more of a comfort zone and if necessary your route home will be easier.

Within your own organisation there will be many different teams and these are worth mapping out. Don't assume that a section or a department represents a team however. Different managers, supervisors, buildings and even rooms may create the opportunity for workers to feel allegiance to a team at odds with the aims of the overall department, let alone the business.

This is a natural process of the way our brain behaves which Dr Edward de Bono refers to as 'centring'. Natural phenomena are governed by catchment areas. A river valley is an example of a catchment area. It does not matter where a raindrop falls within the valley it will ultimately flow into the river. It cannot go anywhere else. It certainly cannot end up in another river. Our minds appear to use catchment areas to ensure that rapid decisions can be made. This analogy is a simplification of the processes going on in our brains but works in the context of the point I am making.

Remember the example of the dinner plate where by seeing it from any angle we are able to recognise it as a plate. The image that we see falls into our 'dinner plate catchment area' and our mind always ends up with the same recognition.

Using spell-check to correct the many mistakes I have made when writing this book is another good example of centring through pattern recognition. Once I received the proof copy I realised that I was over-reliant upon it however. There are some words that I repeatedly get wrong such as strategy, transformation and organisation. On most occasions the spell-checker is able to decipher my errors and suggest the correct spelling. Occasionally though it struggles and gives up.

My jumbling of the word organisation seems to give it the most difficulty for some reason. My brain however makes short work of recognising what the word was meant to be both through its general shape but also the context in which it was being used. According to researchers at Cambridge University, it doesn't matter in what order the letters in a word are, the only important thing is that the first and last letter be in the right place because the human mind reads the word as a whole[22]. I correct the mistake by typing the word much more slowly than normal.

The point is that once something is caught in any catchment area it will be drawn towards its centre and teams behave in such a way. Once someone is part of a team they are drawn towards its ethos and

---

[22] This is how this text first appeared to me: Aoccdrnig to rscheearch at Cmabrigde Uinervtisy, it deosn't mttaer in waht oredr the ltteers in a wrod are, the olny iprmoatnt tihng is taht the frist and lsat ltteer be in the rghit pclae bcuseae the huamn mnid rades the wrod as a wlohe. Spell check could cope with only the shortest of words yet the human brain can read it very well.

behaviours which may end up being in conflict with those of the wider business.

I'm always amazed at the amount of internal conflict in organisations, especially large ones where inter-team rivalry and budget conflicts suggest that different teams are actually different organisations. How many times have you been told that you have come through to the wrong department or that 'they' should not have told you that? Large organisations tend to think about themselves as a collection of smaller teams or departments. Often this approach is encouraged by structures, incentives or unnecessary boundaries and this is exactly where Guerrilla Working can make a big difference.

The idea of creating an internal market is an example of such a divisive approach, one that was designed to improve internal business relationships by making them more business-like but instead encourages unhelpful behaviours. An internal market is where services and functions within an organisation treat each other as though they were normal, fee-paying customers. The idea is that this will engender a sense of competition and put services on their metal as they strive to improve service levels under the implied threat of losing the business to some other provider.

This is a fine notion to improve attitudes toward the 'customer', communications and responsiveness to business enquiries. But there must be a difference between a customer who works for the same organisation and one that does not.

As an example, a car mechanic goes to buy a printer cartridge from a local stationer. The mechanic needs the printer cartridge as he has some invoices to send off, to get the cash in to maintain his garage business. The stationer however, wants to sell the cartridge so that he can trade and build a successful stationery business. The objectives of the two organisations are linked but are completely different.

Now imagine another example. A bicycle manufacturer is large enough to have an internal marketing service and also an internal print service. Here, the role of the marketing department is not in itself to become a leading marketeer, its role is to help the company sell more bicycles. The role of the print department isn't to become just an effective printer, its role is to help the company sell more bicycles.

Unlike external customers, the internal customers should have the same overall corporate objectives as each other. Where the wheel falls off is when internal customers start to argue about cost. If, as in the above example, the marketing service decides that it can buy the print cheaper externally then the internal market can quickly descend into a farce.

The marketing service will spend time obtaining and comparing quotes from the internal and external providers. It will probably need to set up a small team of buyers and administrators to support this. Meanwhile, the print service will have to spend time responding to the quotes and fiddling with its prices to appear cheaper. It too will need to add resource to be able to compete. Valuable management time will be wasted arguing about the merits of trading with each other.

All of this adds cost to the organisation and detracts from the objective of selling more bicycles. This money can only come from somewhere and that must be from the price of the bicycle, making the company less competitive.

Guerrilla Working, by breaking down the barriers between teams and enlarging their catchment areas, allows organisations to create a single brand that supports its overall objectives. Businesses need to work sedulously to break down anything that interferes with the development of their single brand.

Jeff Bezos, Founder and CEO of Amazon.com says that 'Your brand is what people say about you when you leave the room. It's the sum of all the impressions that you, or your business, leave on another person. And the real test of the quality of your brand identity is what people say to their friends, family and colleagues.'

On a recent visit to hospital I made my way to my appointment with my reminder letter in hand, which clearly stated that I should make my way to the department on the first floor. When I arrived the receptionist greeted me warmly and advised me that I had come to the wrong floor. I pretested mildly and showed her the letter and pointed out the line that clearly said that I should make my way to her department on the first floor. 'They're always doing this' she said and added 'I've had eleven people up tonight with the same letter.'

This does not represent a single brand proposition. The word 'they' suggested a separate organisation and the frequency of the wrong letter would suggest that rather than trying to address the problem the approach was to blame some mysterious and incomprehensible administration. An ideal candidate for Guerrilla Working perhaps where the two different teams share their experiences and devise a system that works and presents a united front.

Compare and contrast this with a visit to Tesco, one of the world's leading supermarkets. I visited one of their out of town super stores of around 10,000 square metres and was looking for a tin of baked beans of all things. Finding what you are looking for in a shop the size of two football pitches can be a daunting prospect and so I asked a member of Tesco's staff, who was re-filling a shelf with product, if he could tell me where I could find the beans.

I was expecting him to give me the aisle number but instead he put down the product he was stocking the shelves with and walked me through the store to the very shelf the beans were on. I thanked him profusely, feeling somewhat embarrassed that I had dragged him away from what he was doing, to which he politely asked if there was anything else he could help me with. How easy would it have been for him to have said 'not my department' or waved his hand in the general direction of tinned goods. I was left impressed by the stores willingness to serve its customers and by the extent of his knowledge.

I had a similar experience at John Lewis, a major retailer that is often held up as an exemplar of customer service. I was shopping for a gift for one of my daughters and stopped at the makeup counter to ask if they stocked Bert's Bees products. The assistant said that they did and offered to take me to where they were to be found. I replied that it would be fine if she just pointed to where they were. 'No, that's fine' she said to me, 'It's not my department but I would like to find out more about the products and so we can go across together if you would like.'

In this way the assistant recognised that there were specialisms within the store and that not everyone could know about every product but she saw this as an opportunity to learn. I was not seen as a failed makeup customer but rather a John Lewis customer who wanted to purchase something within the store.

John Lewis is an employee-owned UK partnership which operates the John Lewis department stores and Waitrose supermarkets. All people who work for the business are partners and have a vested interest in its success whether or not it is directly related to their own department or not. For them it is the brand that is most important.

In the above examples I am not saying that the National Health Service (NHS) always gives bad service or is a bad organisation, far from it. The people of the UK are in a privileged position to have widespread access to excellent health care. I am using this as an example of how the NHS does not present the patient with a single brand and is divided into smaller teams with a degree of competition, either intentional or not, that confuses the customer and detracts from the quality of service.

I'm not saying either that Tesco or John Lewis always give good service and if only the NHS could learn from them everything would be better. I have had dreadful service from Tesco when trying to return a faulty television. One of their floor manager's take it or leave it attitude resulted in me having to write to their head office. I can also give examples of where shop assistants in John Lewis have been rude and arrogant.

Good service and bad service are not the exclusive rights of any organisation and all need to be vigilant and keep working away to break down artificial internal barriers. Most businesses have enough competition for new customers, new resources and new employees to have to waste time in internal conflict as well. This is why Guerrilla Working with its ability to uncover talent, increase visibility, create new realities, provoke ideas and to have fun is such a powerful tool in addressing such internal tensions.

So let's get back to the plan. You are starting with your own organisation and have started to map the different teams. The concept of mapping is useful at this stage as it creates an overall view that will act as a frame of reference.

I have referred to the concept of catchment areas earlier in this chapter and would like to expand upon the idea. Imagine a square wooden frame filled with sand that has been smoothed absolutely flat but that rises above the edges of the frame. Water is then sprinkled on from a watering can. At first each drop will create a small indent in the surface of the sand. As more water is added then the indents will grow bigger and perhaps join together. Eventually, once the sand is water logged, the water will start to flow and will cut rivulets into the surface changing the surface for ever. Very quickly the surface of the sand will move from being a flat surface to one with little valleys and areas of 'higher' ground. Any water that is now added is more likely to flow down the already created rivulets rather than open up new channels, cutting them deeper and reinforcing the new landscape.

This is a simple model of how the earth's terrain has been created. The surface of our plant has never been flat however but over billions of years it has been bent out of shape by tectonic forces, deformed by the impact of meteors, added to by molten lava and ash spewing out of by volcanoes and weathered away by running water and ice. In relative terms to the earth, tiny forces over huge lengths of time have transformed our planet into the world as we know it. Small differences in the surface structure have been exacerbated and emphasised to become huge mountains and deep valleys.

In in 1964, Arno Penzias and Robert Wilson, at the Bell laboratories in New Jersey, discovered what later became known as Cosmic Microwave Background Radiation.[23] They were working with radio waves and were having problems trying to remove some background interference. They discovered that this noise was evenly spread in whichever direction that they looked and was always present, day and night. After much further work they eventually concluded that this radiation was coming from outside our own galaxy and in conjunction with other scientists discovered the residual energy from the moment that our universe was created, the so-called Big Bang.

At first it was thought that this radiation was constant in every direction but later, after nine years of microwave data was collated, it was discovered that there were tiny variances in temperature throughout the universe. It is believed that these peaks and troughs or ripples in the energy are what gave rise to all of the stars and galaxies in the universe.

These are further examples of centring and show how very small differences over time can become significant.

All organisations will have started with tiny differences built into their fabric. By their very nature people are different and this will have created ripples in the background radiation of an organisation. Over time these differences will be added to and weathered by forces such as buildings, management, customers and the myriad of individual relationships.

So your own organisation will be highly complex, with continents, high mountains, deep crevices, frozen wastes, scorching desserts and some rolling countryside. You probably already know where the difficult terrain is but mapping the organisation will improve your understanding of how to plan your approach.

---

[23] http://en.wikipedia.org/wiki/Cosmic_microwave_background_radiation

Sun Tzu, the ancient Chinese military strategist dedicated a whole chapter to the use of terrain in warfare in his book 'The Art of War'.[24] He is quoted as saying 'If you know the enemy and know yourself, you need not fear the result of a hundred battles. If you know yourself but not the enemy, for every victory gained you will also suffer a defeat. If you know neither the enemy nor yourself, you will succumb in every battle'

In the Battle of Agincourt the English won by forcing the French across a muddy ploughed field. It had been raining heavily. The Alps have long protected northern Italy from invasion, yet Napoleon Bonaparte and Hannibal Barca both tried to use this to their advantage. During the Second World War the Germans heavily defended the Normandy beaches knowing that that was where the allied invasion would happen. Che Guevara used the dense forests of Cuba to his advantage allowing the element of surprise to be added to his tactics.

Guerrilla Working is not warfare though, it is about all parts of an organisation winning through better understanding of its operations yet strategies and tactics are needed.

We can take it as read that the larger the organisation then the greater the number of teams will exist. It is also generally true that the more dispersed an organisation is and the smaller the individual offices then there will be a greater number of teams. The type of organisation therefore with the highest number of internal teams is likely to be a large organisation with many differing functions spread across a wide geographical area and in old fashioned accommodation. Does this sound like the place in which you work?

As a rule of thumb teams will have a supervisor for every five to ten employees. An organisation of a hundred people will have at least eleven teams, with one chief executive and as many as ten managers each with their own team. The managers will be part of two teams, the one they manage and the one they attend with the other managers. No doubt it is in the latter group where the inter-team rivalry will be encouraged.

An organisation of ten thousand employees will have a number of teams a degree of magnitude greater. Even if it was within one building (which it won't be) and there was a rigid hierarchy (which there won't be) there will be five layers of hierarchy and at least 1,110 different teams each with their own nuances, rituals and sub-cultures.

Of course there will be some teams that are more important than others. A lot will depend upon the type of organisation that you are working in. If you are employed by a car manufacturer then great stall will be set by the engineering and production teams for example. If you work in a bank then security and audit will feature highly in the importance stakes. Be careful though. When looking at the terrain map it may be that the continents are not the most important parts of your organisation. Vatican City is the smallest country in the world with an area of less than half a square kilometre yet its influence and power is global.

Seasonality also has a role to play in making some teams more important than others. If your business deals with schools you are likely to be very busy in term time and less so in the holidays. Toy manufacturers won't be making much around Christmas as it would be too late by then as the goods have to be in the shops much earlier.

Nearly all businesses have a seasonal element which can be driven by external factors such as the weather and legislative change or by internal factors such as financial year end. Revenues and Benefits services in England, that pay benefits such as housing and council tax benefit to thousands of people, have to go off line for a week in spring to allow for the software to be upgraded to accommodate changes in the benefits laws. This causes a false break in activity followed by a surge as the business trues to catch back up.

Marketing will be busy up to the launch of a campaign and then hopefully sales will be busy after the launch. Car sales in the UK used to be driven by the annual change in number plate. Each year a new prefix or suffix was added to the unique number plate causing a surge in sales when the new letter arrived in August. Now new number plates are issued twice a year to smooth out demand.

At Spicers there were two peaks of demand, one in September and one in March. The first corresponded to the start of the academic year and the second to the end of the financial year. To meet this demand, warehouse employees were on annualised hours contracts where they worked longer hours in the busy periods and shorter hours in the quiet periods.

Information without context is meaningless and so it is necessary that you overlay your organisational terrain map with an understanding of the relative importance of each team. At this stage this information will have to be based upon perception, either yours or that of your colleagues, as you have not been out into the field.

Importance though is another amorphous concept. It could mean who has the most influence, access to the most resources or who is doing the most important work. In most organisations the assumption is that the more senior the person is then the more important they are. In truth there will be many more people within the organisation that could influence and change the decisions of their more important seniors. There are senior leaders who have someone else who does their bidding on their behalf. In political environments it could be that some officers hold more sway than the politicians and indeed it can be the other way around.

Individuals or organisations that make donations to political parties will often deny any intention to influence the policies and plans of their chosen group yet they remain very important and the politicians will ignore them at their peril. Shareholders and the electorate may not have much power or authority as individuals but collectively can and should be hugely influential.

Authority and power can rarely be separated from influence. They are directly correlated. The greater the influence, the greater is the authority. In the most successful organisations the ability to influence is understood and is aligned with the needs of the customer and the flow of goods and services towards them. The understanding of flow is useful in understanding influence and the understanding of influence is useful in the understanding of importance. The truly important parts of an organisation are those that are close to the flow of value irrespective of how important an individual or team may think otherwise.

Influence and flow can be very different between commercial or profit making businesses and public sector organisations.

Let's go back to Tesco and my tin of beans. The act of picking a tin off the shelf and paying for it kicks off a chain of demand-led logistics. Once enough tins have been bought than the shelves are restocked from the warehouse within the supermarket's distribution chain. These warehouses are in turn refilled from the manufacturer presumably from their stock in hand which is replenished from their production lines. The production of beans requires a steady flow of raw materials, with some obvious ones such as beans and tomatoes but also tin cans, paper labels and packaging. All of the latter items are themselves manufactured and delivered to the baked beans factory as required.

The act of me buying the beans has created a pull in the demand chain. Clearly I have influence over the supermarket as I am a customer of their products but the supermarket also has influence over me by making sure that it offers products at prices that tempt me into their stores. Likewise the supermarket has influence over the manufacturer yet they also have influence in reverse by making products that customers want to buy. The manufacture has influence over the raw materials suppliers and the story goes on.

In a commercial organisation where there is a clear customer the

demand chain can be said to be linear. In reality there are no straight lines at all but if it was drawn on a piece of paper each of the component organizations could be joined by a linear flow of goods and the corresponding opposite flow of demand. On a tube map it may look like the Northern Line between Morden and London Bridge[25].

In this example I have referred to myself as the customer but there is another important player in this equation and that is the consumer. For the purposes of my argument the customer is someone or some organisation that expresses choice through money, or in other words the customer pays. The consumer uses the goods and services.

In the case of the beans I was the customer as I paid for them but I may not have been the consumer. The consumer has an enormous amount of influence in purchasing decisions. Anyone who has children will know the irrepressible nature of pester power. Many adverts on television are aimed directly at the consumer and bypass the customer altogether. Providing advertisers can get to the children then the parents are going to buy their products.

In the example and in most commercial arrangements the consumer and the customer are very close and are usually related. The vast majority of product purchased in supermarkets is for the family of the customer. The consumer though is just another stop on our straight line tube journey.

In public sector organisations the picture is different. Here the customer and the consumer can be very far apart. Revenues for public organisations come from taxation and so a person in Penzance can be contributing to the welfare of a consumer on Peterhead. Decisions made in Northumberland County Council, England's most northerly council, for example are heavily influenced by decisions made in the Westminster parliament some three hundred miles away.

The relation between customer and consumer is not close and is often

---

[25] http://www.tfl.gov.uk/assets/images/general/standard-tube-map.gif

not straight forward. Rather than looking like the Northern Line, demand within public organisations can look like the whole tube map.

When I was working at North Tyneside Council I developed the ASCC model to describe the complexity of demand flow in the public sector. ASCC stands for Agent, Supplier, Customer and Consumer. There can be multiples of each within a single service and every one of these has influence in most public sector decisions.

Let us consider as an example the case of a looked after child with severe learning difficulties. Who is the consumer here? It is not really the child as they are unlikely to be in a position to make difficult decisions about their future care needs. It could be the parent's but it could also be a foster carer or even the council itself if the child is in care. In reality there are several consumers of the service operating at any one time.

What about the customer? Indirectly it could be argued that it is the parents who are the customer in this case but this may be complicated by the reasons already given in the previous paragraph. The parents may not be tax payers and even if they are it could well be that they have not contributed enough tax to pay for the complex needs of the child. Is the council the customer then? If so it will be both the supplier and the customer and even possibly the consumer of its own services.

The role of the suppliers is obvious but there will more than one. These could include organisations such as care providers, health providers, transport providers and specialist equipment suppliers. In such an example the service will need to be built in a process akin to the manufacturer in the baked beans example, in a process known as commissioning.

The final group I refer to as agents. These are individuals and organisations that do not necessarily have a direct role to play in service delivery but are very influential in the way that it is delivered. There could well be a whole host of agents or agencies involved in the care of the child. Organisations such as the Care Quality Commission[26], the Association of Directors of Children's Services[27] and the Local Safeguarding Children's Board[28] will all have an interest in the way that the services and care are delivered.

Rather than being a linear flow of goods and services from supplier to consumer there is a network of competing demands that act in a network to influence the outcome. The consumer does not have the financial proximity to the customer in order to have the same influence in the commercial model and this lack of direct influence permeates throughout the demand model. This makes understanding a public sector business more difficult as there are many more opportunities to influence and consequently to be ignored.

Of course no one can hope to be able to understand a business or organisation in its entirety. Even the smallest of operations will be a chaotic mix of feelings, emotions and abilities yet it is useful to have at least laid down some perceptions of how the land lies. At this point your perceptions are good enough as facts are hard to come by. I would argue that there is no such thing as the truth, just perception and probability. I may perceive that I am a good singer but the probability of me being right is very low.

Your time is precious and so should be targeted at those areas which will have the greatest of impact upon whatever criteria you consider to be important. The terrain map that you perceive is overlaid with the relative importance of each team and the hierarchy of people within them. You have set this against the flow of goods and services and corrected for any seasonal issues and so you are all set and ready to go.

All of us are very busy yet it is important that we manage to set time aside to realise the benefits of Guerrilla Working. I've already remarked that we reward our best people by giving them more work. We do this

---

[26] http://www.cqc.org.uk/
[27] http://www.adcs.org.uk/
[28] http://www.safenetwork.org.uk/training_and_awareness/pages/lscbs.aspx

because the best people get through it and make things happen. We come to rely upon them and so if you are busy then you must be good.

But remember that work is a thing that you do and not a place that you go. You are busy because you have lots of things to do and not because you happen to be in the office. How much of your work can be done anywhere? As long as you have the things to hand that you need, and we recognised in chapter 3 that this wasn't very much if you have an office based role, then being busy is not an excuse for not being able to get from behind your desk. Indeed somewhere different might be the refreshing break to see you through that big virtual pile of paperwork. A change is as good as a rest. Consider it as a holiday – a 'workation' perhaps.

Any time when you could be working by yourself in your office could be spent anywhere. Only when others are involved does the location need to be specific yet this can be used as an advantage. Having to go to a meeting at a specific building affords the opportunity to work in that location before and after the meeting. Alternatively having a meeting affords the opportunity to get the whole team to meet somewhere unusual instead.

Discipline is required. Your diary has to be considered and used as a tool to plan your forthcoming locations. If you are due to meet some colleagues in a different department then the day can be focussed around their teams. If they are not on your important or influential list then use the physical move to work with teams you have identified close by. This begs the question why you are meeting with colleagues who you have decided are not important but perhaps that's for another book.

Keep tabs of where you have been and where you are going. You could just turn up and work but you will find that you end up in the same teams time and time again. Rather than becoming a Guerrilla Worker you will just become a multi-site worker with a favourite docking station in every building.

Much of what we do we do without conscious thinking. Have you ever been driving and wondered what happened for the last twenty miles, or arrived at a destination that you had not intended to go to? Do you find yourself parking in the same spot in the car park more or less every day?

People who are right footed when crossing the road and approaching a kerb will unconsciously shuffle their steps so that they always step onto the kerb with their right foot. Try it next time you are out and try to step up with your left foot. You'll feel better for it.

Without a conscious effort to break our patterned behaviour we will do the same things over and over again. By keeping a record of your target teams and when you visited or when you are planning to do so you will ensure that your precious attention is spread to the best effect.

My team at Durham County Council works out of several sites and from several different rooms in each building. I keep a list (electronically of course) of all of the different places along with the date of the last time I went and called in even if it is just to say hello. By sorting this list in date order those sites that I haven't blessed with my presence stand out like a sore thumb. I can then go back to the diary and set some time aside to make amends.

Even with this list there are still some places that I don't go to as often as I should as they are just a little off the beaten track. Once again Guerrilla Working can help. One of the sites is at Crook which isn't very far away from where County Hall is but it is not really on the road to anywhere else that I would go and I have only a few colleagues there. To me these sound like excuses and actually they are because at the same location there are several other significant groups of people which is why some of my team is based there. This gives me the opportunity to work in amongst these people while visiting my team which only adds weight to the guilt I am feeling in not going there as regularly as I could.

Don't forget about those workers who do not keep regular office hours. Night-shift workers are often overlooked when considering teams to get involved with. Whilst not very common in office environments the global nature of trade and the extended service hours that we have come to expect will mean that many people are working outside of the nine to five. Retail is a seven day a week activity and the emergency services run round the clock every day of the year. In the UK over a million people are at work on Christmas day. Good ideas, team working and opportunities to learn about the business don't stop at the office door.

Finally for this chapter we need to consider how to break the ice with our new colleagues. Imagine how you would feel if your boss suddenly appears, sits down next to you and starts working? The first thought would probably be along the lines of 'what have I done?' Is he or she coming to check up on me or is there something specific they wish to raise?

Would it feel any better if someone equally as senior but you were unfamiliar with did the same? This could well be worse. You may feel that they have been sent to spy on you or that they are going to take over from your current boss and they are getting the lie of the land. It could be that they need a special favour from you or want to push into a work queue to get special treatment. Whatever the reason you are going to feel suspicious and be on your guard.

Picture the scene which happens in reality. It's early on a beautiful spring day. The sun is rising but the dew is still clinging to the lush green grass. A colony of rabbits is happily grazing when a fox appears. The first rabbit notices the fox, the biggest threat to rabbits and raises the alarm. Awareness runs through the group like a wave and soon all of the rabbits are sitting upright with their muscles tense ready to run. Suddenly the fox is on the move and makes a dash for one of the creatures. Panic sweeps through the colony as rabbits run everywhere. White scuts are on display in an attempt to confuse the fox but he is too wily. The caught rabbit squeals as it is captured. The fox has made a kill. Almost immediately the rest of the rabbits stop and get back to eating the grass. The threat is no longer there as the fox will only kill one of them.

People will view anyone new in their midst with a degree of intrigue, uncertainty and suspicion at least until they feel that any threat is diminished. It is important therefore that any Guerrilla Worker shows common courtesy and respect for their colleagues' working environments. Remember that you are the invader and it is up to you to try and diffuse any tension.

Start by introducing yourself, ask if the desk is free and would it be alright if you were to work there for a while. By all means explain what you are doing there rather in your own space but don't jump in with too many questions. Start working as if what you are doing is the most normal thing in the world as it soon will be.

Blog entry: Working from home

Agile working is great but it is not always plain sailing as I find out from time to time:

Working from home is a mixed blessing. You can get a load of things done but there are just too many distractions, especially when there is someone else in the house with you.

Working from home isn't something that I do a lot of officially but of course if I count the unofficial stuff then I guess it is something that I do almost every day. But sitting down at the kitchen table with my laptop open and notebook at the ready is quite a rare experience for me. I do it when I have to go somewhere which is closer to home than work or need to catch a train or an airplane and there is some time to kill before it departs. At other times I work from home if I have a big report to write and I don't wish to be disturbed.

The good thing about working from home is that you are not distracted by your work colleagues and you can choose which bits of technology that you switch on or not. People will find it harder to reach you as there is a psychological barrier between them and you because you are not at your work place. If you are working from home it must be important and you don't want to be disturbed, right?

The bad thing about working from home is that you have to stay focused as there are so many distractions, a cup of coffee and a biscuit, something from the fridge, the Jeremy Kyle show on the television. This is made much worse if there is someone else in the house that can distract you and keeps popping in to ask you if you want a cup of coffee and a biscuit or to tell you what is on the Jeremy Kyle show. If it is their home as well then there is no psychological barrier between you as you are on shared turf. If you are working from home it can't be that important and you don't mind having a chat, right?

Then there are the strange dilemmas in that you can stop working at work and not feel guilty but if you are working from home and stop for a minute then you are consumed with guilt. When you are working from home you will often start earlier and work later and by working from home first thing you can avoid the morning rush hour.

There are things that you can do from home such as writing reports, catching up on email or reading lengthy documents. Some jobs are really suited to working from home especially if they are rules based or transactional in nature and can be done on screen. On the other hand though there are things that I find difficult to do such as making phone calls (they seem to be more intrusive) and of course meeting up with colleagues and customers.

This morning I worked from home as I had to go to the airport. I caught up with my email, wrote a couple of short reports, had a cup of coffee with a biscuit but avoided watching Jeremy Kyle (was he on this morning?) To be fair, I didn't chat that much and so I must try it more often.

Widen your circle of influence

So far we have looked at how you can prepare yourself to become a Guerrilla Worker but work is a team sport. No one can be a success all by themselves.

Richard Branson, the serial entrepreneur and founder of the Virgin group of companies, Mark Zuckerberg, the founder of Facebook and Indra Nooyi, Chief Executive Officer and Chair of PepsiCo are fabulously successful, at least in monetary terms. Whatever you think of them as people they have to be respected for their enthusiasm, energy and creativity. But they did not get to where they are alone. Each relied upon their teams to create the organisations they lead.

Sole traders who run their businesses out of a corner shop or a market stall still rely upon their supply chains and customers to make a living.

Leonardo da Vinci's Mona Lisa is just oil on a poplar panel without those to view it an appreciate it.

Guerrilla Working is a team sport as well. It is about showing that truly flexible individual and group working is possible and sustainable through the deliberate mixing up of people and teams, bringing talent together wherever it matters to solve issues and create opportunities.

With Guerrilla Working, groups of people come together drawing on their own experiences, developing new levels of understanding, building relationships and laying down new knowledge that can be used in addressing future challenges.

It requires different teams of people to come together, not in a passive way but in an active and supercharged way. The Joint European Torus[29] emulates the power of the sun on earth by colliding superheated hydrogen atoms in a process called fusion. The resulting energy released is enormous. Guerrilla Working is team fusion. The greater the energy in the more impressive will be the output.

Saul Kaplan in his book 'The Business Model Innovation Factory' [30] talks about the need for disruptive innovation. In response to a question posed at the Economic Development Forum in Detroit in 2010 which asked 'Given your experience, what are the most 'game-changing' ways to use a significant amount of grant funding ($100 million +) to change the trajectory of an urban economy?' he responded with 'if we want to change the trajectory of urban economies we should start by changing the trajectory of our conversations.'

Guerrilla Working is about bringing people together in new ways and creating the spark that changes the conversation trajectory. It is like the catalyst that causes or accelerates a chemical reaction.

Kaplan also talks about taking ideas off the whiteboard for a spin in the real world. Guerrilla Working addresses this the other way round. It is about taking ideas from the real world based upon direct experience of working alongside the people who do.

When I worked at Spicers, the office products distributor with warehouses all over Europe we would joke about the stereotypical differences between the people of each country. We would recognise those behaviours which conformed to those views probably because we

---

[29] http://www.efda.org/jet/
[30] http://bmif.businessinnovationfactory.com/

were looking out for them. I remember laughing at being told by a Frenchman that the English would say 'It works in theory but does it work in practice?' whereas the French would say 'It works in practice but does it work in theory?'

Whether this is true or not doesn't matter. The point is that people are products of their environment. Their experiences will influence the way that they view the world. Their perceptions will be their reality and so having people from different backgrounds can challenge our assumptions. There are many universes out there waiting to be explored.

Next time you are in a newsagent pick up a copy of Model Rail Magazine and you will enter into a parallel world in miniature. For some the pictures within will remind them of their childhood with Hornby 00 tracks and engines spread out in an imaginary world on the bedroom floor. For others it will conjure up images of men of a certain age who should know better. If you ever go to one of the many model railway exhibitions that are a regular feature of leisure centres and town halls across the country you'll find out just how very popular a pastime it is.

As you read the articles you will find that the modellers refer to the prototype, the landscapes that they use as the basis of their models. They replicate them in minute detail, romanticising them and capturing them usually in a bygone age which never really existed. What they call the prototype, we would call reality. Their model works in reality and they try to replicate it in a different context. The reality has come before the theory.

Guerrilla Working allows us to experience work practices and ideas in practice before considering them in theory. Taiichi Ohno, the father of the Toyota Production System would make a point of moving machines on the production floor to highlight that change need to be made. He changed the trajectory of convention and of conversation to develop a new paradigm. He started with reality, what was happening in practice and used an intervention to move from one perception plane to another.

Mineral extraction started off as a surface activity. Gold was found at the bottom of streams. Being heavy the lighter silt was washed away leaving the shining nuggets behind. Gold rushes would start when the metal was found by panning in the mud at the bottom of streams. Today very little gold is found this way. Most is extracted by digging gold bearing rocks from the ground. It takes approximately 10,000 times the amount of ore to create a quantity of pure gold. One ounce will also take 5440 litres of water, 572 kilowatt hours electricity, 12 cubic metres of compressed air, lots of dynamite and tons of chemicals to extract.

Coal extraction started in a similar way by being exposed through land erosion. This led to drift mining and eventually deep shaft and open cast mining as seams became more and more difficult to follow.

Opportunities for change and improvement within organisations may at one time have been lying on the surface waiting to be gathered but that won't last for long. They are more likely to be hidden in seems and nuggets beneath the surface. As Saul Kaplan puts it 'The best opportunities to create value will be found in the grey areas between silos, sectors and disciplines.' Again Guerrilla Working allows workers to be on the ground looking to dig out those rich and valuable possibilities.

Not all change occurs in big chunks however. Much will take place in small differences that add up to create something innovative. Dave Brailsford, General Manger of the British cycling's Team Sky refers to this as 'the aggregation of marginal gains' and he has used this technique to achieve unprecedented success in both track and road cycling.

Brailsford says. "It means taking the 1% from everything you do; finding a 1% margin for improvement in everything you do. That's what we try to do from the mechanics upwards."

"If a mechanic sticks a tyre on, and someone comes along and says it could be done better, it's not an insult - it's because we are always striving for improvement, for those 1% gains, in absolutely every single thing we do."

The traditional approach to project and programme management has been to start by identifying senior people who can get involved in the project team. Suitability for this team is normally based upon seniority or longevity and a balance is struck within the membership to make sure that all interested parties are represented.   But the word interested comes to mean doesn't want to be left out. Many project team members will want to be there just to keep an eye on the decisions that are being made and to ensure that their own interests are represented.

A senior responsible officer is chosen to sponsor the change and a project manager is appointed along with senior users and suppliers. Note the word senior which leads to a project or programme group being populated by people who have achieved a certain position within the organisation and have probably not done the work that their teams carry out for some considerable time.

Senior managers are not necessarily appointed because of their prowess in the function that they come to represent. A supermarket manager will not be the best baker, check out assistant or shelf stacker. They will have become the manager because they have the ability to lead, hopefully, and have the drive and stamina to compete with all of the other candidates who would have wanted that job.

Because of this the project or programme team becomes filled with representatives chosen because of their position or younger pretenders who understand their points of view. By its very nature the team is divorced from the actual work and the theory is put before the reality. This is one of the reasons why so many projects fail and why so many workers who have to live with the changes know they are going to fail from day one.

The Service Desk at Durham County Council was suffering from a deterioration in service levels. Outstanding work queue lengths were increasing and telephone response times were getting longer. Whilst senior management were able to hypothesise on the reasons, or guess as it is probably better known, a quick discussion with the operators who answered the telephones gave a list of half a dozen reasons why the deterioration was happening. They were confident that the cause was a small number of one off incidents that had led to higher volumes than normal and sure enough within a few days volumes and response rates had returned to within normal expectations.

There is no substitute to experiencing reality.

Guerrilla Working brings people together into existing work environments to develop ideas and apply creative intelligence to real environments. This would have allowed senior management to get a first-hand understanding of the changes on the Service Desk.

But is this not just Agile project management in another guise? Agile is about managing projects to deliver outcomes more quickly and more effectively. Agile project management and Guerrilla Working are not the same but are not exclusive. Guerrilla Working uncovers issues that haven't been seen before or that haven't been challenged. Agile project management addresses known issues that need to be changed. Guerrilla Working could highlight areas for improvement which Agile project management could be used to resolve.

The UK Government Digital Service[31] uses Agile to manage very successfully all of its projects and uses discovery to gather the relevant data. Their blog says that 'Asking for information of busy people isn't enough. Getting the right regular forums in place to gather data for clear purpose has better success. We added a weekly meeting (called the GDS Approvals Board) where we ask one simple question of the senior management team: Based on the information we have, should

---

[31] http://digital.cabinetoffice.gov.uk/

this project move into the next stage?' Agile uses discovery to draw information away from where it is created to somewhere where it can be processed to deliver better products. Guerrilla Working allows the information to be viewed in context and in action.

Guerrilla Working uses techniques similar to a Hackathon which brings programmers and software developers to collaborate on software projects in an intense and focussed environment. Hackathons bring opportunities to a group of people brought together specifically for the occasion whereas Guerrilla Working gathers people around opportunities that exist within the place of work.

Sometimes referred to as hack day, hack-fest or code-fest , the Hackathon events last for a short and hectic period fuelled by pizza and beer. The word hack in this context refers to exploratory programming in a fun and playful way rather than the criminal act of trying to break into other organisation's systems.

The idea behind a Hackathon is to present the group with some back ground information about a particular subject and to let the members collaborate to create software that solves issues or creates opportunities depending upon the individual skills and perceptions of the participants. Prize money is sometimes made available to add an element of competition.

Some significant companies have been born from Hackathons such as GroupMe, which was later bought by Skype and PhoneGap which was eventually bought by Adobe.

The City Of Manchester held its first Hackathon in November 2011[32]. Hackers, coders and creative collaborators were invited to dig underneath its digital skin and help shape the future of the digital city. Manchester was looking for experts and innovators to hack, code, programme and experiment with the city's sets of open data to build new applications and develop future services. Participants were let

---

[32] http://futureeverything.org/

loose on data sets provided by a range of public sector partners and were asked 'to produce anything they wish - develop applications to help people find their way around, stay safe, discover new experiences and everything and anything in between.'

Entries from both teams and individuals were welcome and cash prizes were offered for the best product at the end of the session, including a grand prize of £10,000. The winner of the FutureEverything Award 2011 was Macon Money by Area/Code. Macon Money is a city-wide social game that crosses between the real world and online social media to try and solve problems around segregation

A Hackathon is about seeing new ways of delivering something through new perceptions. Having unusual data sets, unusual in that the hackers are not used to seeing them, allows perceptions to be formed freely and without fear of being non-conformist. Being non-conformist is the very point. Mixing data sets allows patterns to be seen that had until then been hidden away. How many opportunities and new ways of perceiving things exist within our own data sets? How many opportunities exist within the current ways that our business is delivered?

Changing people's perceptions is difficult as you are dealing with both the way that the mind works and social norms. Everyone knew that the Emperor was naked but everyone saw his new clothes.

My wife likes to watch the history channel and is fascinated by any programme to do with the ancient Egyptians. They are of less interest to me but I find myself drawn to the hieroglyphs carved in to the stone structures. I know that each cartouche means something and that each glyph adds a sound or a meaning to the word or phrase but I cannot read them. They were finally deciphered in the early 19th century by Jean-François Champollion and now there is enough online help to make anyone an expert.

I have the same problem with any script that is not Latin script, such as

Chinese or Arabic. I can recognise the symbols as letters and words but cannot read them.

I have the opposite problem with anything that looks like English or any western European language. I cannot help myself but try to read them. I cannot not read. Have you ever tried not to read? It's impossible as far as I am aware. Once you have learnt how to recognise the individual letters and how to construct the phonics and form words it is impossible not to see a script and read it. This is how the brain works through pattern recognition.

Aristotle, the Greek philosopher and polymath, said that all new knowledge came from existing knowledge. This is only partially true. New knowledge requires a degree of empirical understanding, is difficult for example to do mathematics without an understanding of arithmetic, but real break throughs come through a shift in perception rather than a layering of knowledge.

I have already argued that all facts or truths are really only perceptions and probability. Facts and truths can be altered by changes in perception. Nicolaus Copernicus changed the perception of the way that the universe was ordered, although there are claims that this had been realised much earlier. He changed perceptions by moving the Earth from the centre of the universe to a heliocentric model where it circled the Sun. We now know that the Sun is just another celestial body in a much more complicated structure.

Science is the systematic knowledge of the physical or material world gained through observation and experimentation. It is knowledge, as of facts or principles, gained by systematic study. Breakthroughs in science again come through changes in perception. Indeed many scientific discoveries lead to further questions and paradoxically as our knowledge expands the so does our lack of understanding.

Real change can only come through perceptual shifts. Some of the things that we take for granted now only seem realistic in hindsight such as the Post-it note which uses a non-sticky glue or the smartphone that takes photographs. The knowledge of glue didn't create a glue that didn't stick. The knowledge of mobile phones didn't create the fusion with camera technology. Today more photographs have been taken on mobile phones than all of the photographs that went before their invention.

Steve Jobs, the co-founder and former chairman and Chief Executive Officer (CEO) of Apple created a new market for music by changing the perception that recorded music came on physical medium to digital. His vision and its subsequent realisation have transformed the recorded music market completely creating a whole host of me-too products and competitors.

The British Broadcasting Company completely changed the perception of the game of snooker by using it as a mechanism to get viewers to convert from black and white television to new colour sets. Snooker uses different coloured balls and is almost impossible to follow if you are unable to recognise the differences. On the back of this the popularity of snooker soared and the ironically named television programme 'Pot Black' was one of the BBC's highest rating shows for many years.

Donald Rumsfeld, the American politician who served twice as Secretary of Defence under two separate presidents was widely mocked for saying that 'There are known knowns. These are things we know that we know. There are known unknowns. That is to say, there are things that we know we don't know. But there are also unknown unknowns. There are things we don't know we don't know.' Yet he was right. Our knowledge is what we know and we can use this to find out things that we know that we don't know but not to find out what we don't know we don't know.

Imagine there is a room where you work that you have never been in, which is locked and that nobody you know has ever been in. No amount of knowledge about the rooms that you do know about can tell you anything about what is in the locked room. You will be able to guess, or form perceptions through hypotheses about what it may contain. You may be right. But there will be people who have been there and will know.

Guerrilla Working brings people together with different experiences in a dynamic and exciting way. Its high energy impact allows new perceptions to be realised and these act as catalysts for a shift in the way that the business is delivered.

Bringing people together creates a greater opportunity for ideas to be created from changes in perception. The relationship between the number of people and the number of ideas however is not a linear function but rather a factorial one. Bring two people together and there are not two points of view but three, each individual and the combined views. Bring three people together and there are six possible combinations of opinion and perception. Four people create twenty four and it goes on.

Of course as the number of people gets too large within a group then the ability to interact decreases and so the effective combination of perceptions stalls. This is similar to the Laffer curve which represents the relationship between the rate of taxation and government revenue. Initially as the tax rate goes up so does tax take but eventually there comes a point where the tax rate is so high there is no incentive to produce more and more incentive to avoid tax and eventually tax take decreases. You can't get too much of a good thing but clearly you can. Vitamins are good for you but in too large a quantity they become poisonous.

I have already described Guerrilla Working as the deliberate mixing up of people and teams, bringing talent together wherever it matters to solve issues and create opportunities. Groups of people come together drawing on their own experiences, developing new levels of understanding through different perceptions, building relationships and laying down new knowledge that can be used in addressing future challenges.

It is going to be hard if not impossible to do this alone. You need to get others involved and the best place to start is with those people who you can influence. This is going to depend upon where you are in an organisation. People you manage directly, team colleagues, people in your peer group or those you just get on well with are all good places to start with. Here are a few ways to widen your circle of influence:

Get your team into unusual places

If you manage people then you are going to influence this group much more easily. They are already looking to you for guidance and leadership and will take a cue from your actions. Think about how you can get your team into unusual places and situations that take you all out of your comfort zones.

You can start to find out what life is like in the other parts of where you work by moving meetings around on a rota basis and by going to places where your employees or customers are working. There will be meeting rooms that you can use which are outside of your normal work area. If your organisation is large then there will be many of them that you don't know. Each team will have a space that they go to and each separate building will provide new opportunities.

Try using senior manager's office if they are vacant as they are normally big enough to accommodate meetings. If they are not vacant, try asking them if you can kick them out for a while. This will certainly test how ready they are for Guerrilla Working. Even better, ask then to join your meeting and start the way you mean to carry on. They are bound to be able to add something of value.

I heard Paul Theroux, the American travel writer and novelist, speaking on the BBC Radio 4 programme Bookclub about how people described where they lived. They might say that they lived in London for example but he pointed out that they didn't live in the whole of London, just a very small part of the city. In the same way we might say that we work for an organisation yet in truth we are more likely to work only for a small part of it.

The very act of going somewhere different will create a freshness in the approach of the team. A change is as good as a rest and having different scenery or fixtures and fittings to look at could be the very catalyst needed to change perceptions and create new ideas.

People act differently when they are on holiday. They take their time, do things that they enjoy such as getting round to reading the book they have had on their bedside table for the last six months. They stop and have a cup of coffee when the mood takes them and they go on excursions.

But why wait to go on holiday to have new experiences when they are all around. You can act like you are tourists in your own organisation. Imagine you are on a workation.

Remember the map you developed in chapter 4, with all of its continents, high mountains, deep crevices, frozen wastes, scorching desserts and rolling countryside. Get it out and plan your journey with all the exciting places that you are going to visit. Stop and look at the marvels your company has to offer. See things in a new light. You might even want to take some photographs or souvenirs to remind you of your trip.

Make sure that you and your team are visible and don't waste the opportunity by slipping unnoticed into a meeting room somewhere out of site. Say hi to the natives and take an interest in what they are doing.

If you don't manage a team directly then suggest some of these things to the people who do.

Encourage others

To make Guerrilla Working a reality it needs to be part of the strategic discussions that you have as a team. You should take every opportunity you can to make it part of your vocabulary and encourage people to talk back to you about it.

There is nothing more human than a story. They are a very powerful way of getting your messages across and I will cover their use in a later chapter. You should weave your Guerrilla activities into the stories you tell and repeat those that others tell you. Good stories have a character, a reference in time and an outcome that can be recognised. Guerrilla Working can give rise to many good stories because of the people you meet and the places that you go.

Give the subject a regular slot at management or at face to face meetings that you chair or that you attend. It is a rich source of inspiration and insight into the way that your business or your customers operate.

Your own team is only part of the equation however. Even the largest team will be around a dozen people. Anything larger and the group will split itself into smaller inner-teams. So by concentrating on team related activities only your influence will be limited.

We have all heard of the theory, originally put forward by Frigyes Karinthy known as the Six degrees of separation where everyone in the world is a maximum of six steps away from each other. In this way everyone knows someone, who knows someone, who knows someone etc. and the whole world is connected.

For example, I know a colleague who knows a person who worked for Morgan Tsvangirai (Changerai), the one-time Prime Minister of Zimbabwe who clearly knows Robert Mugabe the President of that country. In this way I am only four steps away from Mr Mugabe and we're nearly acquaintances.

In a similar vein I have met several of our local Members of Parliament who will have met Tony Blair, who in has met many of the world's leaders including the Queen and the Pope. So I'm even closer to the

Pope than Robert Mugabe.

And while I'm on the subject, the nephew of Tony Jacklin, the English golf player and winner of the Open Championship and the US Open, fitted a new boiler in our house.

The serious point here is that whilst we may not have direct contact and influence over very many people, we know people who do. Even in a very large organisation it does not take many contacts to be able to get a message to any individual employee. If each of us, for example only new six unique individuals within six steps we would be able to cover more than 46,000 people.

In order to generate interest in Guerrilla Working therefore and to spread the word the best approach is to encourage your near neighbours, those individuals that you can influence, to talk about it and promote it with their influence group.

One of my first jobs was selling parts and paint to the automotive aftermarket. It was a very influential time for me. I recall my sales manager telling me that it takes five times the effort to sell to a new customer than it does to an existing customer. I doubt that the mathematics could ever be done to ascertain whether or not this number is correct but the sentiment rings true.

It is much easier to sell to someone who has already bought from you. They have already expressed that they like your products, are satisfied with your service and have a relationship with you. In the same way it is much easier to influence those who you already have a close relationship than those who you don't know.

You should spend your effort encouraging those you work closely with to encourage the people that they work closely with. In this way you will widen your circle of influence and be able to encourage more people.

Of course the best way of encouraging someone to change their behaviour is by acknowledging them and supporting them when they work in a way which fits in with the intended approach and highlighting it to the when they don't.

Imagine if you had to teach a child to walk by sitting them down and taking them through a set of instructions: stand up straight and try and distribute your weight on both legs; lean your torso slightly forward; shift your weight onto one leg; using the leg that your weight isn't on raise the foot off the ground and move it about half a leg length forward; bring your foot to the ground and shift your weight onto that leg; repeat with the other leg; continue until you reach your destination at which point; bring both legs to a similar position and start from the beginning.

How successful do you think you would be? It would take you a life time to explain what each of the words meant before you eventually got around to the process of walking.

It is far better to do what humans have done since the dawn of time and that is to hold out your arms and say encouraging words to the child until it launches itself at you and makes its first tentative steps. You then tell them how clever they are, even if they made a complete mess of it, and get them to try again and again until they are quite good at it.

As Samuel Beckett put it 'Ever tried, ever failed, no matter, try again, fail again. Fail better.'

This method of learning requires trust. The child needs to trust that the parent is going to be there to catch them should they fall and the parent needs to trust the child that it is going to make the effort.

Sugata Mitra has put this practice to great effect with his School in the Cloud experiment[33], which has brought self-organised learning techniques using the internet to children in remote and developing

---

[33] https://www.theschoolinthecloud.org/library/resources/the-school-in-the-cloud-story

parts of the world. Children get to explore the questions that matter to them as they receive encouragement from 'Grannies', volunteers who can drop in over Skype to spark the children's curiosity and help make learning happen.

Encouraging people to take up Guerrilla Working requires similar levels of trust. The manager needs to trust their employees to be working on what is expected of them when they are out of sight and the employee needs to trust their manager that they will be looking out for them and support what they are doing. This can only come through meaningful relationships that allow the build-up of a mutual understanding.

Trust takes time to develop. It is most likely to develop when things go wrong as this tests boundaries and expectations. It also allows people to see how others will react in such situations and whether or not they really believe in what they are putting forward.

Any parent with young teenage children will understand. At this age they are too young to be independent from their parents but are too old to remain fully dependent upon them. Relationships between parent and sibling will be strained as the teenager tests the boundaries and limits to their growing freedom and their parents' resolve to contain them. The child will come in later than told, go further than they are allowed, hang out with people and do things that are expressly forbidden while their parents wonder where they have gone wrong. The mobile phone has certainly gone some way to helping parents keep a safe eye on their children but only adds to their woes when it is not picked up instantly.

I am not suggesting that employees should be perpetually testing their manager's resolve but that mutual trust should be built in order that everyone understands the level of independence and direct dependence required. I will come back to this in a later chapter.

Talk the language of your colleagues

When I worked at North Tyneside Council I was telling a friend of mine how I had great difficulty in explaining to colleagues about some issues that I had to deal with and how they could be affected. I was finding it hard to get my point across and speak to them in a way that meant something to them. I did not feel that they had an understanding of a bigger picture and my efforts to make them aware were lost. I really could not understand why they could not see my point of view and didn't automatically know the 'right' thing to do.

My friend, she is called Victoria, listened intently as I explained the multiple methods I had used to communicate and the tricks I had employed to make a difference but that it had all been in vain. She nodded her head in empathy and asked 'Have you ever taken them to lunch?'

This simple comment stopped me dead in my tracks. Suddenly I was able to see where I had been going wrong. I had been talking to my colleagues as an outsider, from my perspective and without any real understanding or sympathy for their position. So I took my friends advice and met with each of the people that I needed to deal with over lunch, individually. We talked about many things, mostly about work but in a much more open and friendly way. All of us have a life outside of work which affects our approach whether we believe it does or it doesn't and sharing lunch was a great way to start to get to know each other.

From these lunches I was able to glean an understanding of their values and what motivated them about their work. I was then in a position to describe my issues in a way that they could picture and appreciate. It took some time to get around all of the team and some lunches were less enjoyable than others but overall it was a worthwhile strategy. It certainly was good advice.

We've all heard of the expression 'a family that eats together stays together' and it's true of your colleagues. I use the technique still today and often meet the management team to which I belong in the staff restaurant to have lunch. Our topics of conversation are varied, from hobbies to holidays and from weekends to, quite naturally work.

In The School Food Plan[34], Henry Dimbleby and John Vincent found that teachers eating with children lead to improved behaviour and education attainment.

They describe how 'In every school we went to that had a good food culture – every single one – the teachers regularly ate lunch with the children. One of the best meals we had was at the Reach Academy in Feltham, south west London. The children sat at long tables, family style, with teachers scattered among them. Before the food was served, one of the teachers stood up and gave a short speech – almost like a secular grace – about the delicious meal we were about to enjoy. The food was then brought to the tables, and one child at each table was given the task of dishing it up.

At our table, a group of year 7 children (several of whom had come to Reach after struggling at other schools) chatted to a teacher about what they would like to study at university. After lunch, a senior teacher stood up and thanked the cook for the food that had just been eaten. It was a wonderful example of how the dining hall can set the tone for the whole school, encouraging kindness, civility and a sense of togetherness.'

If you really want to be able to work closely with someone then it's a good idea to get to know them as a person rather than just a work associate and that eating lunch together is a great place to start.

But you need to make sure that you share a common language. I've been trying to learn a foreign language for as long as I care to admit. I wish that I had tried harder at school because the older I get the more difficult it becomes. I've got by in French, dabbled a bit in Italian, German, Swedish, Icelandic and Portuguese. I have even managed to learn a few words in Esperanto, the great language hope for a united Europe.

---

[34] http://www.schoolfoodplan.com/plan/

But my greatest though relative success has been in Spanish. Over time I have passed a GCSE, followed by an AS level and now continue to polish my linguistic skills by trying to read novels in my adopted tongue.

I have a problem though and it is not so much the Spanish but the types of books that I insist on reading. The more challenging for me the better and most of the books that I battle through would be a challenge, I think, even in English. I understand the words, I understand the sentences and the paragraphs but the strain of reading something in an unnatural (to me) language means that I struggle to understand the story. At times I get the plot but at others I lose the bigger picture and the reading becomes a slog. I want to press on, I've got many pages left but I have to go back to pick up the thread where it snapped.

I deliver a lot of presentations in the course of work, including to the whole of the ICT Services every other month. The Senior Management Team has also held some feedback sessions on some engagement work we have recently completed. Whilst these have gone to plan from my perspective and are well attended, it is obvious that only some of the messages we are trying to get across are sticking. The team seems to be blissfully unaware of some of the things it should be aware of.

Could the problem be that I am using a different language? Could it be that I am using management speak in which I appear to be fluent (probably more fluent than I would like to admit) and they are struggling to keep up the translation in their heads. I'm sure that they understand the words, the sentences and even the paragraphs but is it the story that they are missing?

Benny the Irish Polyglot[35] is convinced that anyone can learn a foreign language and be fluent in three months. I came across his site when I got the urge to learn Dutch for some reason, perhaps with a view to going on holiday there and was looking for some inspiration, something

---

[35] http://www.fluentin3months.com/

to get me started.

His method for learning so quickly is simple if a bit brutal. To be fluent in a foreign language you have to stop speaking English. By forcing yourself to use the foreign tongue you learn from your mistakes and you are empowered by your successes. All language started in speech and all people learn to talk though listening and copying others' speech. So, no more text books, no more CDs that you listen to in the car, no more getting hung up on tense and grammar, just getting on with it and muddling your way through to success.

It is an approach that he has used many times with great effect. A month of absolute discomfort leads to near fluency within three months.

And this is an approach that we can apply at work. How many times do we fail to be understood? How many situations have we been in where both sides have put forward their arguments but no agreement has been made? How many times does it seem that we are speaking a different language?

If what Benny says is true (I have no doubt that it is) and the best and quickest way to learn a language is by immersing yourself in it without the protection of your mother tongue then the best way to be understood and get an understanding is to leave your own language behind and immerse yourself in that of your colleagues.

Language plays a fundamental part in the culture of an organisation or the teams within it. If you want to be accepted and get to know them better then stop using your own jargon, live among the natives and use only the language that they understand. This is an important point. Language is only part of our culture and so perhaps we need to learn to live in all aspects of others' culture.

I hope this is not too patronising, it is certainly not meant to be but in management you become very used to talking in the abstract, the conceptual and the strategic whilst the rest of the team is more used to talking in the immediate, the practical and the operational.

If this is the case (and I suspect it is) then I need to try harder to get my messages across, not through better communication but through better engagement and by demonstrating concepts and strategies through practical and operational examples. I need to learn to speak their language so that they don't have to stop to go back and pick up the thread.

Change in an organisation is limited by its ability to absorb the change and so our messages should concentrate on fewer but better messages rather than more conceptual ideas.

But it is not just language that needs to be common. Working in Information and Communication Technology it is somewhat ironic that the industry is accused of speaking in a language of its own that no one else can understand. The belief is that it is designed to keep the uninitiated out. A big criticism comes over the use, or rather the misuse of jargon. Now all industries have their jargon and by using it you can reinforce your membership of the group you belong to. It seems though that the ICT industry has a reputation second to none.

Jargon needs to be avoided or when this is not possible, explained.

Different groups of people also use the same word but in a different context. I still recall the look of confusion on my boss's face when I said that we were planning to do some work around a Christmas cabinet. He thought I was referring to the Council's decision making body, the Cabinet, when I was referring to a green box at the side of the road. I was actually referring to a DSLAM (Digital Subscriber Line Access Multiplexer) but this would have thrown both of us.

ICT people talk about resiliency and redundancy with specific meanings when talking about machines that are different to other common uses of the words. I might talk about unemployment, resources and the elderly but my colleagues will talk about worklessness, capacity and older people.

I've already asked why wait to go on holiday to have new experiences when they are all around. You can act like you are tourists in your own organisation. When you are on a vacation you can try your language skills out on the residents of the country you are visiting. Giving a foreign language a go is often appreciated. It shows that you are willing to make an effort to understand their culture.

You can do the same on a workation by trying out the language of the service you are visiting. I'm sure that making such an effort to speak the language of your colleagues will be equally appreciated.

Don't be afraid to manipulate

I spend most of my time at work trying to get the best people into the jobs that they are best suited to, creating situations that allow them to be stretched and develop while trying to clear the right paths to make this happen. Guerrilla Working helps.

Most people would call this manipulation but that is such a horrible word. It suggests that what I am doing is somewhat underhand and deceitful and that I am trying to manoeuvre people into doing things that they don't want to be part of and somehow tricking them.

The word manipulate is pregnant with negative meanings and condescending connotations. It sounds like I am man handling people and pulling them into things that they don't want to do yet it didn't set out this way.

The word is a back formation of manipulation which can mean skilful or artful management. Apparently it is from the Latin manipulus which gave rise to maniple (in ancient Rome) a subdivision of a legion, consisting of 60 or 120 men, literally, handful, equivalent to mani- (combining form of manus hand) + -pulus suffix of obscure origin; perhaps akin to plēnus full. The word manipule, meaning a handful, such as of grain, comes from the same route.

Yet getting people into situations that make the best use of their skills and that marry their talent with opportunity cannot be a bad thing or can it?

A good hostess at a party will make sure that her guests are enjoying themselves. She will go around topping up glasses, making sure that everyone has something to eat and that no one is without someone to talk to. She will skilfully introduce people who she believes will get along, those who may share a common background or interest and will spark up an interesting conversation. A good hostess will skilfully manage her guests to make her party good. She will manipulate them.

A good chess player will try to make moves that outwit his opponent. He will be prepared to lose some of his pieces with the aim of drawing his opponent into a trap, making him expose his king so that he can win the game. This is what the rules of the game are designed to do. It is the mental stimulation and strategic thinking that is required that makes the game so interesting and that has guaranteed its survival over millennia. A good chess player will trick his opponent. He will manipulate them.

Enter into a supermarket and you will be greeted by the smell of fresh bread. It is a pleasing smell that is redolent of being warm and secure and will put you into a good or at least a better mood for the shop ahead. The smell is piped from the bakery at the back of the store to just near the door as you walk in. The first part of the store that you enter will be the greengrocers, with racks of inviting vegetables, fruit and staples such as potatoes and onions. The greengrocery is first because there is a very high chance that each customer will need to purchase something from this section and once you have something in your basket you are up and running. If you buy one thing then you are likely to buy another and another and so it goes.

At every turn in the supermarket you will be targeted with tempting offers to get you to buy more produce. Ends of aisles will have bulk offers. Eye level shelves will have the products that people will most want. Impulse purchases will be placed amongst the basics and everyday items. Even at the tills you will be tempted by a final packet of sweets or a magazine.

The supermarkets do this in order to increase their profitability. That is the name of their game. They try to manoeuvre their customers to increase their spend. They manipulate them.

Manipulation is something that humans do to each other all of the time. We are both manipulators and manipulated.

Just like a good party Guerrilla Working allows people to meet new people. It allows people to meet people they already know but in new ways. It allows them to build relationships in the most human of ways through face to face contact.

Guerrilla Working is a challenge to all of the procedures, practices and tenets that are holding current organisations together but are in fact holding them back. It helps organisations to make the best use of the enormous talent that is locked upon inside their employees, their customers and other stakeholders.

If this requires a little manipulation then it has to be worth it.

Show some humility

Very few people like to be first yet someone has to be. Nobody likes a clever clogs but someone has to add challenge.

When faced with difficult and challenging circumstances most people prefer to look inward rather than outward. They look to the status quo rather than the new. Adapting to Guerrilla Working is new and can be difficult and challenging for many people and the last thing that they want is someone who is cocky, arrogant and appears to know it all.

Some humility is required. Your colleagues will need some latitude as they are going to make mistakes and become disgruntled along the way. I've used the analogy earlier of teaching a child to walk. They learn through trial and error with a healthy dollop of encouragement.

Making mistakes is part of the process. We learn to walk by falling on our behinds.

The same is true of everything that we do. Master craftsmen would take on apprentices as they would trade their skill and experience for some willing and low cost labour. The apprentice knows that the skilled worker will teach them their craft by pointing out their errors and helping them to correct them.

Many entrepreneurs have failed in their business ventures. Many successful people have been sacked from previous jobs. Failure and perhaps more importantly learning to learn from failure is a key to success. As Henry Ford put it 'Failure is simply an opportunity to begin again, this time more intelligently.' Humans can be funny creatures and sometimes we judge an organisation by how it responds to problems rather than the on-going quality of its service.

When I worked at Spicers, I was visiting a customer over in Cumbria who spent a certain amount with us but the bulk of his spend was with our main competitor. I asked him what it was about the opposition that made him prefer them to us. He described how they had a good relationship with Bill, their local representative. I felt sure that we could form just as good a relationship and so I pressed him a little more. Apparently there was nothing that Bill wouldn't do for them. 'If ever they make a mistake with a delivery such as something is missing or it's the wrong product then we get straight onto the phone to Bill, he throws it into the car and drives across to sort it out,' the customer said. 'Well wouldn't we do that as well?' I asked, to which he replied 'I don't know, you never make a mistake.'

It was the fact that there was a deep empathy for Bill that built a loyalty towards him and in the customers eyes this was more important than a more efficient yet apparently colder service.

People admire modesty, manners and self-deprecation when it is appropriate. Going into their turf with all guns blazing could be construed as arrogant and off-putting and you will have an uphill battle to get them to engage and develop new and shared experiences. A little humility can go a long way.

Blog entry: MOT tests

One of the biggest issues with working in ICT is that there is always more to do than the resource you have and, because of this it tends to be the big things that get worked on. People don't bother reporting the small stuff and over time they get used to coping with niggling problems on their computers or find work-rounds when with a little help and guidance they could have them resolved. They would be happier as there would not be the constant thorns in their paws. The ICT Services would be happier as people would be getting more out of their technology and the organisation would be happier as productivity would improve (as would employee satisfaction).

It is just a matter of too little resource, or is it? Perhaps not, instead it may be a question of rearranging what resource we have and using it more effectively and that is what we tried with a piece of group Guerrilla Working which became known as an MOT after the annual Ministry of Transport test to make sure your vehicle is roadworthy.

The idea was to descend upon a service, start at one end and work our way through the room asking questions, giving advice and fixing those pesky problems. We didn't need an excuse to get this started but the approach of National Customer Service Week seemed to be too good an opportunity to ignore. This series of events is run in the second week in

October, and provides a week long opportunity for service and support professionals across the UK to recognise the important role that customer service plays in every organisation and what better way to demonstrate this with our MOT.

As this was our first attempt we chose a friendly service to work with and worked closely with the Manger of Operations and Projects within the Human Resources department. A small team of ICT colleagues spent a day within the main HR open plan office at County Hall helping with and addressing:

- Any ICT related problems or queries they needed support with;
- Handy hints and quicker ways of doing things;
- How to save documents in a more structured way;
- Maximising the use of ICT, providing new ways of more effective working.

The day was a great success as the HR Manager Operations and Projects, said "We had excellent support throughout the whole day provided by a small team of professional and helpful ICT staff. They visited every team within the HR Service and responded to a range of queries from individuals and groups of staff; this included solving issues with mobile phones/PCs, tips on how to maximise ICT to streamline processes, general advice on excel and word as well as providing their own suggestions on how they could assist us. A very worthwhile event and we would welcome similar in the future – thank you to all involved".

The issues we got involved with were ones that people would never have bothered to raise with us and it was only because we got in and amongst them that we made a difference.

Making it real

In Julian Barnes' novel 'England, England' Sir Jack Pitman says that sometimes you can only do something by doing it. This is true of Guerrilla Working. There is no substitute for getting on with it.

In chapters 3 and 4 I described how you could get yourself in a position to be a Guerrilla Worker. In chapter 5 I looked at how to get a wider group involved and in this chapter we are going to put our plans in action and the only way to do this is by doing it, walking the walk and talking the talk.

Remember that we are setting out to change the world by engaging with new people and bringing new experiences and perspectives to problems and processes. Your insights will be invaluable and you will learn from the shared experience of the teams that you 'invade'.

Plan your attack

You need to plan your attack. Dig out the one you prepared in chapter 4.

Identify the objectives that you are trying to achieve. Is there a group of people that you want to get to know better because they are influential or essential to the core business? Is there a process or a function that you need to understand better that being onsite would help? Do you think there is an area in which your insight or different approach would be of help? Is there a part of the organisation which you know nothing about but feel you should?

Which team are you going to start with? You should do your homework and gather information about them in advance if there is any available. Have they published a strategy or a service plan or a customer charter for example?

Does anyone in your team know them already either through work or socially. Wherever I have worked there has always been someone who knows everyone in the organisation. They have usually worked there a long time and have been in a central role that covers all of the functions such as in payroll or procurement. Find out who they are and ask them about the target team.

Guerrilla warfare is the deliberate use of small and highly manoeuvrable troops with a sound knowledge of the terrain to wear down larger and apparently more organised armies though the element of surprise. It may seem rough and ready but its tactics are not accidental.

Guerrilla Working is the deliberate mixing up of people and teams, bringing talent together wherever it matters to solve issues and create opportunities. It may look and feel chaotic but it is not accidental.

Get the lay of the land. Take a look at where they work. Have a scouting trip to their office and find out how many desks there are and how many are free at any one time. What are the facilities like? What is the mix of people in the office like? How is the hierarchy arranged in the office, such as does the manager have a separate room, are the different teams located together. How manoeuvrable can you be?

You're going to appear in their theatre and start to work as if it is the most natural thing in the world to do. After all, it is. To work is a natural human activity. You will be engaging with your target group and creating some excitement, some new ideas and some new ways of working. You'll be cats among the pigeons. You'll come in a flurry of excitement but be ready to melt back into the undergrowth when it's time to leave.

And don't forget your provisions.

Choose your team

Remember that Guerrilla Working is a team sport and that a team is made up of several people. You should think about the team that you intend to go into battle with carefully. The best teams have individuals with different characteristics and approaches who can bring different perspectives to a range of problems. A team should be built for a specific purpose or individuals within the team should lead depending upon their view point and the needs to be addressed.

We would expect that optimism and enthusiasm are the characteristics most needed in business and in life but this is not so. Sometimes there is an obvious need for caution or reflection.

Primo Levi, an Italian Jew and chemist, has published many books about his imprisonment in the Nazi concentration camps during World War II. In this extremely tragic period in history it was his view that it was the pessimists that were the most likely to survive the experience, if that is not too small a word to express their ordeal. Those who started out as optimistic were always looking for sanity to break out and for their confinement to end in a matter of days. They would always start their conversations with soon or tomorrow or not long now. Levi noted that they could just not keep this up and after a while would give up, become inwardly focussed and that their end would follow shortly.

On the other hand the pessimists would 'accept' that the way things were was the way that they were going to be and that a white knight was not going to suddenly appear to rescue them. In a situation that they could not alter or influence it was better not to waste the effort but rather to focus on survival by any means.

This is an extreme example but makes a point. Having a team of the same kinds of personality makes as much sense as having a toolbox filled with screwdrivers only. It is impossible that the team that you intend to work with will be made up of the same kind of people anyway and facing them with the approach would be a wasted opportunity.

When a football manager selects the team he, or increasingly she, is not just setting out to win. Instead he is setting out to beat the team that they are due to play. All football teams are individual and present a different level of threat and so the manager needs to set his own team accordingly.

The players need to be robust in defence, visionary in mid-field and good in front of goal. The opposition may be stronger on one side or another. They may have more pace down the left wing or have greater skill down the right. They will have a number of star players that will need to be marked more closely than perhaps the rest.

The manager will need to make their choice depending upon injury problems, levels of fitness, match readiness while trying to balance the need to bring fresh players through the ranks. They will have three chances during the match to change the shape of the team if things aren't going as planned by using substitutions. And they have to do this week in, week out in front of thousands of supporters baying for success under a constant threat of dismissal, especially in the upper leagues where failure can costs millions.

Sporting analogies don't always translate well to business where the players are on field for days, weeks, months and years at a time rather than a fixed ninety minutes. In sport the rules are clear before the teams compete and there is a referee on the field to make sure the players comply, whereas in business the rules change constantly with competitors and customers looking to gain a competitive edge.

But team selection does translate and an understanding of the people you intend to engage with is worth having. Skills such as the ability to engage with people easily and naturally, or the ability to interpret what people are saying (talk the language of the customer), or the ability to analyse complex business processes and articulate them in simple diagrammatic forms or the ability to read the underlying political climate and identify the key players in a given situation are among those which should be considered.

You may even need to take along people who do little other than watch and listen. When you are not very well and in pain it is always best to take someone else with you when you go to see the doctor. Your suffering clouds your ability to concentrate and understand whereas a relatively dispassionate observer will be able to recall much more of what the doctor ordered. The same is true of any stressful situation but can also be true of times of high concentration.

Staying in the moment takes effort and having a wingman (should that be wing person?) can be an advantage. The term comes from the military and refers to the practice of flying slightly behind and to the side of the lead aircraft in a formation. The job of the wingman is to watch the back of the lead pilot.

Guerrilla Working is the deliberate mixing up of people and teams, bringing talent together wherever it matters to solve issues and create opportunities and so having the right people on the team will matter, not just right for the team but right for the people you are going to engage with.

Decide on your tactics

You have identified the characters that you hope to be working with as well as you can and set up your own team in the best way to meet the challenges ahead. You have also agreed the outcomes and objective that you are looking to achieve, the why, and so what needs to be done now is to decide on tactics. Who is going to do what, where and when?

Is the Guerrilla team going to stick together and arrive as a single unit or are they going to split up and work as individuals or in pairs. The answer will depend upon what it is that you are trying to do.

In my working life I must have been to thousands of conferences and training events. It never ceases to amaze me how few people use such events to mix with other teams across the organisation. After all it is an ideal opportunity as everyone is out of their natural environment. Nearly all delegates will sit in their own team structures or with their immediate circle of work colleagues. Before such events I would take the opportunity to sit down with my team and agree who would sit with whom and you would find one of us with each of the different groups. This is an example of what I mean by choosing your tactics.

Our tactics would be based upon such considerations as who knew which other team's members, who had a better understanding of their business drivers or simply who wanted to get to know that team better.

If the aim of your Guerrilla Working is to improve the understanding of a business function then spreading the team out evenly across the whole office and comparing notes later may be the best approach.

If the aim, however, is to get a much deeper comprehension of a specific part of a complex operation than having the team together and observing the same things from different perspectives might be more appropriate.

If you are looking to improve the knowledge of the team you have engaged with about your own service then it might be best to focus on solving specific issues or teaching specific skills. The Human Resources team could use such a technique to help people understand a new policy for example or the Information and Communication Technology team could do something similar to improve basic ICT skills.

It may well be the case that the best laid plans will go out of the window as soon as the enemy, or rather the opportunity, is engaged but having some understanding of the structure of your approach agreed in advance will keep your campaign on mission.

Work on perceptions

Jill Bolte Taylor is a scientist who studies the anatomy of the brain, a neuroanatomist, who points out that 'Although many of us may think of ourselves as thinking creatures that feel, biologically we are feeling creatures that think.' What humans feel or perceive about something is much more important than what they think. Thinking about a person or a situation can take time. You can mull over the options and convince yourself that your logic is correct but what you feel is almost instant.

This is an evolutionary response to give you that extra fraction of a second to escape danger. Having to think about every response would cost you your life. In complex vertebrates, including humans, the amygdalae, sometimes known as the lizard brain, perform primary roles in the formation and storage of memories associated with emotional events. This is an ancient part of our nervous system

The expression 'You only have one chance to make a first impression' is a reminder of the point. Perceptions can be formed in an instant and take a life time to be changed.

Henry Ford said that 'Whether you think you can, or you think you can't--you're right' and the same is true of how people perceive you. If they think you're up to no good then that is their 'right' and it's going to take a huge effort to convince them otherwise.

The Richard Dawkins Foundation sets out to support scientific education, critical thinking and evidence-based understanding of the natural world in the quest to overcome religious fundamentalism, superstition, intolerance and human suffering. Yet you can't disprove belief through logic.

Edward de Bono's 'Six thinking hats' creates a simple mechanism to break down the act or process of thinking into manageable chunks and directions. The premise is that there are six thinking processes that can be used independently to give a better insight into any problem or issue. Each is represented by a coloured hat which the thinker can wear to focus their train of thought or to indicate to others in their group of the current thinking style. A yellow hat for positive, green for creative, white for facts, black for negative, red for emotion and blue for control.

The use of the red hat, real or virtual, allows people to say what they feel about a subject rather than what they think. It is very difficult to beat belief using logic. When expressing thoughts it is often necessary to fix a position that can be argued and arrived at logically. Beliefs do not require such a logic. Instead they are just heart-felt and using this technique can move groups from a position of apparent conflict to a position of consensus.

People can see conspiracy in everything and can read nuance into any situation. Just before the Good Friday agreement was signed in the late nineties, I was in Northern Ireland and was speaking to a colleague about the yes / no referendum. On asking if he intended to vote yes he paused and responded 'That depends what you mean by yes.' Clearly life in Northern Ireland at that time was not binary.

No one is binary in their outlook. Even the most ardent black and white person can chop and change their mind depending upon how they feel about something.

In his seminal book 'Emotional Intelligence: Why it can matter more than IQ' Daniel Goleman describes how humans have 'two minds'—the rational and the emotional. Appealing to the rational is never enough and you need to focus more on the emotional. If people were predominantly logical then there would be no religion.

Learning to engage with someone on the emotional level is much more important than on the emotional. Start by showing some empathy and don't forget that at first the people you join are going to treat you with suspicion if not scepticism.

Develop shared experiences

Guerrilla Working has to be good for everyone involved. It needs to be good for the activist and it needs to be good for the team in which they are embedded. It needs to be a win win campaign. To achieve this we need to concentrate on developing shared experiences.

Guerrilla Working is about mixing things up, bringing people together with differing experiences and creating alternative perspectives in a fun and exciting way.

Experiences can come in many guises.

An experience can be a particular instance of personally encountering or undergoing something:

On an ordinary day my commute takes me between fifty minutes and an hour but on one particularly wintery day it took me five hours to get home.

The snow had started to fall in the early afternoon. I watched through the window as the sky grew heavy with a silvery pink light, watched as the lightest of flakes started to drop from the heavens and watched as the view was completely lost in a white veil. I thought I would need to get off home early to avoid a difficult journey and rushed the meeting through to make my escape.

The drive was uneventful at first. The traffic was heavy in all of the usual places and I thought nothing of it until I got to the bottom of the bank at the southern end of the Team Valley and saw the stationery traffic curving away in front of me. It was then that the traffic came to a grinding halt.

The following four miles or so took me the best part of two hours, stopping and starting, five or ten metres at a time with not long enough between times to turn off the engine. I tuned in to the local radio station to get some traffic news and was advised that there were problems due to snow and ice (not very helpful) and that Lobley Hill was closed due to a lorry blocking the road (more helpful). I inched my way along in the worst traffic jam that I have ever been in on that stretch of road, though not the worst jam I regret to say that I have ever been in.

The radio was my companion and I hopped between channels hoping to glean some news that would help me out of the predicament. Eventually I was able to get off the A1 and work my way over the relatively quiet Scotswood Bridge to re-join the A1 a few miles further on and finally north of the Tyne but it was stop start all the way up the long drag to Kenton Bank Foot. Another hour had passed by the time I got to the brow of the hill and it was then that I discovered the cause of all the delay.

The road that fell away in front of me passed Great Park and towards Gosforth Park was a sheet of ice like an Alpine glacier. Tyres had no grip and the vehicles were moving by the force of gravity alone. For the first time that I could remember I was afraid to be driving. I gripped the wheel, waited my turn until there was a large gap between me and the van in front and edged my way over the lip and down the incline. It was almost impossible to control the car even at the two or three miles an hour that I managed to hold but eventually, after what seemed to be three lifetimes, I had reached the bottom of the hill and was able to pick up the pace to a more comfortable twenty miles an hour.

I have been along that stretch of road hundreds, thousands of times but I have never seen or been on anything like it. It was not a patch of black ice but a two mile frozen river polished to a sheen by the cars and lorries on their precarious journeys. No wonder the road had been backed up. I was never more glad and relieved to get home and felt thoroughly drained by the tortuous journey. It was a terrifying experience.

My eldest daughter was also stuck in the same jam but half a mile behind me. We kept in touch by mobile phone and so we had a shared and memorable experience.

An experience can be the process or fact of personally observing, encountering, or undergoing something or things generally as they occur in the course of time.

My first real job was selling parts and paint to automotive garages in the county of Oxford. I had started with the company as a management trainee and thought that I was well set to take on any challenge. I was young and self- assured.

My new manager took me into his office and gave me a brief overview of my new role, the patch and the approach to take. He then explained that he had to go out that morning to a meeting but that if I followed behind him in my car he would point out some of the calls along the way.

This was not exactly the kind of introduction I was expecting but I was keen to get started and we both got into our separate vehicles. We headed off to Kidlington just north of the city and sure enough his hand appeared out of the window and pointed at the garages as we passed.

After a while I let him get away and I pulled into the forecourt of the first ever customer I was to visit in my own. I enthusiastically picked up my bag of samples and looked forward confidently to my first large order. How hard could this job be?

The stores man came out to see me, I explained who I was and he suggested, to my utter amazement, that I should leave and not darken his doorstep again, or words to that effect. I was shocked. I hadn't prepared myself for rejection and hadn't thought that there were customers out there that didn't like my company.

I had to think quickly, after all it was my first call and so I explained I was new to the job and if he would be kind enough to explain to me what the problem was I would try and get it resolved. He warmed up a bit and told me about a product that he had received incorrectly a number of years ago that we had refused to take back and refund.

I asked him if I was able to get this resolved would he be prepared to deal with us to which he begrudgingly replied in the affirmative. By this time he was testing my resolve and was as interested in seeing how this would end as I was. I grabbed the offending product with its invoice and sped back to the depot to get a credit note. I appeared back in the garage after about forty five minutes and he was as good as his word. I came away with my first order.

This was the start of my sales experience which has stood me in good stead throughout my career. I shared my experiences with my fellow sales colleagues, there were three of us and we learnt a lot from each other.

We had a shared learning experience.

Experience can be the knowledge or practical wisdom gained from what one has observed, encountered, or undergone: You can be a person of experience.

I have over thirty years of management experience behind me. I've drawn upon the collective wisdom of thousands of others knowingly or unwittingly and I have applied this knowledge and understanding to my work. At times there is no substitute for experience. Every day I still come across things that are new to me but I am able to draw upon those things that have happened in my past to find a resolution.

If you add up the collective years of experience in an organisation it can be enormous. It is approaching 6,000 years of direct working experience within my own service. What an enormous asset this is and one that people are eager to pass on, that's why we take on apprentices. If you want to know what you do then you should try teaching someone else about it. Skilled craftsmen make their work look easy. Much of this is their innate skill but a lot is down to their vast experience. There is a lot of value within this experience.

Experience can be the totality of the cognitions given by perception; all that is perceived, understood, and remembered.

I love to go to the theatre. I would go three or four times a week if I could. I like the anticipation as we settle into our seats, the buzz of the crowd and the hush that falls as the curtain rises. I like the way that the story unfolds and how the actors project their emotions. I laugh at the funny bits and rub my eyes at the melancholy. I especially like the way that the theatre draws your mind to fill in the bits that cannot be portrayed. Getting an aeroplane onto a small stage would be a problem yet I saw Evita get off one as she returned from her trip to Europe. Four people sitting on boxes became a train carriage in 'The 39 Steps' and I always cry when it snows in the Nutcracker.

I particularly like to go and see musicals and ballet. Each to their own but for me the theatre is a great experience.

On the other hand I don't enjoy the cinema. I find the soundtrack too loud, the picture too much in my face and there are people everywhere talking and eating nachos. I very rarely go as, for me it is not a good experience. Even though it is very much cheaper than live theatre I find the cinema to be poor value.

In the Experience Economy, James Gilmore and Joe Pine[36] describe how work is a theatre and every business a stage. They argue that the way to reach your customer is to create an experience with them.

Guerrilla Working is a way to reach out to colleagues and customers in a way that shared experiences can be created. By being in amongst the team, where value is being created then experiences can be built and enjoyed together.

Make it multi-platform

If you are a sports fan you may have subscribed to Sky, the satellite broadcaster and be able to watch a range of exciting sporting events through your television. I like sports and have Sky but have never subscribed to their sports channels as I fear that I would end up watching television all day.

Sky has been an innovator in television sports production over many years and has helped to create global sporting brands such as the English football Premier League. Manchester United shirts are worn almost everywhere in the world, you see them on international news

[36] http://www.strategichorizons.com/intro.html

stories all the time.

Now Sky's products are available through PCs, tablets and smart phones. Sky Sports can be experienced when you are on the move or away from your television. As a viewer you are no longer restricted by your location and you can get the same, if perhaps smaller, experience that you would enjoy at home. They have gone multi-platform.

At one time media channels were independent of each other. A movie was seen on the big screen and a television show was available on the small screen. Now there is a huge cross over between media channels and platforms.

Harry Potter, by J K Rowling, started out as a series of books and has been translated into an enormously successful series of films. These have given rise to a plethora of spin off items including video games, Lego characters and a version of the classic Cluedo board game. You can even see the magic of The Wizarding World of Harry Potter™ at Universal Orlando, take the Warner Bros studio tour in London or visit Harry Potter World in Watford.

Harry Potter is a multi-platform experience and it is the same for many successful franchises. There is a 007 after shave for men who want to capture the essence of James Bond and there are Star Wars figurines for those who prefer a quieter life.

Creating a multi-platform experience allows a wider range of people to enjoy a product than would have been attracted by a single dimension.

Guerrilla Working isn't about being a grand production, quite the opposite but multi-platform is a useful metaphor. People operate on different levels and rely on their different senses to learn and develop. Some people like to read, some to be spoken to, some to use pictures. Using only one platform or one set of methods to engage and communicate will not achieve the objectives that you have set out to.

To engage your colleagues or customers and create alternative perspectives in a fun and exciting way requires us to develop multi-platform experiences using all the tools and techniques at our disposal.

Anyone who has driven any distance on the motorways of England will recognise the green and red trucks that belong to Eddie Stobbart. They are very distinctive and are always immaculate, as are their drivers. Each cab has a different name written on the front just under the windscreen and it can be a fun pastime to spot the names as you drive past. There is an Eddie Stobbart fan club and there has been a television series about the drivers' antics. You can also buy merchandise in the firms' colours including miniature articulated trucks, pens and lorry shaped slippers.

Eddie Stobbart started out as a haulage firm delivering goods by lorry but now they provide logistics using a wide range of transport options including air and rail. They refer to this as multi-modal distribution through which they can cater to almost everyone's logistical requirements.

Guerrilla Working isn't about logistics and distribution but multi-modal is a useful metaphor. Just as Eddie Stobbart meets the needs of its customers through a variety of distribution options then we must use a range of tools and options to develop new levels of understanding, build relationships and lay down new knowledge that can be used to address future challenges.

Highlight the good stuff

There is nothing that binds people together better than having something to moan about. In England we seem to be particularly good about it. We moan about the weather, the service we get, the price of food, delays on the trains. You name it and we'll mutter under our breath about how bad things are.

It's terrible, it's disgusting, somebody ought to do something about it but it's much easier to complain or blame somebody else than to take responsibility and do something about it.

Talking about others' misfortunes shamefully makes us feel better about ourselves. The Germans even have a word for it – schadenfreude which is the sense of satisfaction or pleasure derived from other people's misfortunes.

Talking with your colleagues about how bad the service is from another team makes your team feel better. At least we are not as bad as them. They haven't got a clue what they are doing. I'm surprised they manage to get anything done. Have you heard what they have gone and done now?

Everyone's job can seem easy until you experience it and this is where Guerrilla Working can be of enormous insight and benefit. The deliberate mixing up of people and teams, bringing talent together wherever it matters, allows us to create and share common experiences while developing new levels of understanding about the problems that different teams have.

I have already described how corporate structure can have the effect of exacerbating differences between teams and actually encourage unhelpful inter-team rivalry. If we are, by design, pitched against our neighbouring teams to somehow out-perform them then it will be only natural to feel some satisfaction at their struggle.

To be a truly successful organisation requires all aspects of the business to be focussed on common goals rather than wasting time highlighting rifts within.

Highlighting differences brings people together and highlighting how bad things are somewhere else detracts from issues closer to home. This is a trick that politicians use all of the time. Focussing the public's attention away from a domestic issue and onto an international issue can relieve the pressure on the policies at home. But it can backfire.

Back in early 2002 under the Tony Blair Labour government, the 'spin doctor' Jo Moore and transport department press chief Martin Sixsmith both had to leave their jobs allegedly after Ms Moore sent out an email as New York's twin towers were burning, suggesting that 11 September was a good day to "bury" bad news[37].

The problem was highlighted in Ms Moore's resignation letter to Mr Byers, which said: "Clearly there are some individuals in the department who are not prepared to work with me and are even prepared to invent stories about me as they have done this week."

Yet if we look around at what goes on at our work and in our lives on a daily basis we can see that there are many things that go right. They are just not as interesting to talk about, or are they? Learning to fight the temptation to highlight the negative but instead to focus on the positive is a challenge that is worth the effort.

As the Sam Cooke song goes:

You've got to accentuate the positive
eliminate the negative
Latch on to the affirmative
But don't mess with mister in-between.

Good news is everywhere, you just have to look. I was once at a local coffee shop, one of the lesser known national chains and was eating a panini when my eldest daughter said that she thought there was some mould on the bread. We looked at it and sure enough it didn't seem right. I took it back to the counter. The assistant apologised profusely and said they would make me another one. Happy with their response I sat down and waited for it to come. A couple of minutes later the manager came across with my new panini. He apologised once again, gave me my money back and a voucher for a free cup of coffee.

I was delighted. The business had managed to turn around what could have been a very embarrassing and potentially costly situation into one where I, as the customer, was very happy with their service. I even went up as we were leaving him to thank him for his response. Of

---

[37] http://news.bbc.co.uk/1/hi/uk_politics/1823120.stm

course the real point of this story is that I have told everyone and this warm feeling about their business will be spread far and wide.

The purpose of Guerrilla Working isn't to become part of the team you are visiting but rather to mix experiences and create new perceptions and opportunities. Joining in with the gossip will allow you to become 'one of them' but the aim should be to steer the conversation around to the good things to be gained by working together.

I will look at the power of stories in the next chapter but they are very powerful tools in helping to build a picture of positive benefit rather than a more negative collective. New perspectives can be created by enhancing impressions of both parties using stories of positive activities. Focussing on the good stuff does not come as naturally as indulging in the negative gossip but is much more rewarding in helping to building common goals and objectives.

Learn from what you have done

Guerrilla Working encourages groups of people to come together to draw on their own experiences, develop new levels of understanding through different perceptions, build relationships and lay down new knowledge that can be used in addressing future challenges.

But all of this doesn't happen in one take. Some missions will go very well and the learning will be about the interaction and the activities of the teams. At other times mistakes will be made, opportunities will be missed and wheels will fall off.

The demands of work are constantly changing. The only thing certain is change whether it is through competitive pressure, legislative change or technological innovation. The work place and the people in it need to adapt constantly to these changes and to do this we need to be receptive to learning and development opportunities at all times.

But people are busy. There is always too much to be done to take time out to learn. When most people are asked if they have had any training they think about the time that they spent in a classroom environment with somebody paid to teach them. The assumption is that learning is an activity separate to work which is patently not true. Most training takes place in work, on the job by watching and experiencing things as they happen. Apprentices are taken on to learn from the experienced members of the work force. There is no real substitute for experience.

Learning must be part of the DNA of any organisation. In the good times effort must be focussed on improving process for when more difficult times come along. If you don't, the business is going to be caught out. In tough times preparations must be made to benefit from the up-turn in fortunes when it eventually comes. If you don't then other competitors will take advantage and steal a march on you. Yet in so many organisations training and development are some of the first things to go when belts are tightened.

Successes are an important opportunity to learn and one of the key things to be taken away from any Guerrilla mission must be to step back and learn from what happened. What went well? What techniques worked? Who did we manage to engage with?

Mistakes are also an opportunity to learn. What went wrong and why? What techniques were less successful? Who needs to be encouraged next time?

The most important thing to learn however is the detailed objectives and purposes of the team, the various players that make up the team and how the different experiences within the Guerrilla group can help change perceptions and create new opportunities and experiences. Again learning is a team sport with experiences enhanced by sharing across the group.

Any lessons need to be fed back to our new found colleagues in a multi-platform way. New stories can be told that enhance the positive attributes that have been uncovered and can mine further seams of opportunity.

Create a new willingness

Guerrilla Working starts with teams that are apart with different aims, objectives, experiences and understandings, teams with different cultures even but it ends up with common aims and objectives, shared experiences and greater understanding. Ultimately Guerrilla Working will lead to the same culture across the whole organisation.

Most people will help out a mate, a family member or a neighbour. Fewer people will help out a complete stranger. Modern organisations are organised around small teams of people which are then grouped into larger functions, departments and services. Everything about an organisation, consciously or not, is designed to reinforce the feeling of belonging to your team. Management is team based, budgets are team focussed and targets are set at team level. All of this ends up setting one team against another.

Some healthy competition is good is what we are told but not when the competition is to win the precious resources of the parent company at the expense of other parts of the same organisation.

The Volvo Car Corporation experimented with car production through small teams at its specially designed plant at Kalmar[38]. Opening in 1974 the aim of the plant was to improve quality and output by having a well-trained and motivated workforce that would commit long-term to the plant.

The Kalmar plant stood all of Henry Ford's assembly line practices on their head. Instead of a line with workers doing a single or small number of jobs as the car went past, teams of workers would build stages of a vehicle's construction before passing the part-assembled work to the next team. Job demarcation, whereby only certain individuals could do specialised work was done away with along with

---

[3838] http://www.akesandberg.se/wp-content/uploads/downloads/2010/05/Enriching-Production_Ake-SANDBERG-ed.-1995-2007.pdf

much of the management hierarchy.

Each team, which had between 15 and 25 workers, was given a set of tasks to do before they could pass the vehicle on. It was up to the team to decide who did what and in what order. All they had to do was complete an agreed number of units per day.

The idea was that by working in teams each worker would feel a greater sense of ownership and responsibility. They would be able to express their creativity rather than be treated as robots. It followed therefore that attendance would improve as you would be letting down your mates rather than the company and you would be exposed to peer pressure to perform.

At first the Volvo experiment seemed to work as productivity soared. The company planned to take the next step and get teams to produce whole cars and planned to build another plant at Uddevalla for this purpose. However the concept eventually turned sour as more and more of the production resource became locked up in inter-team conflict resolution and stress management.

The Kalmar plant closed in 1994.

By working in teams each worker did feel a greater sense of ownership and responsibility. The problem arose as the team arrangements encouraged workers to create a loyalty to their team rather than to the company. Success at a lower level was achieved at the expense of the overall objectives of making higher quality and lower cost vehicles.

In many ways the setting up of guilds achieved the same thing. A guild is an association of craftsmen or merchants that is set up on the pretext of improving and maintain skills but in reality is there to control access to tools, materials and opportunities in a way the ensures the financial welfare of its members. Being a member of a guild is good for you if you are a craftsman. You get more work, you can charge a higher price and you are able to control supply. Because of this a member of a guild will naturally do whatever is best for the survival of the association which may be at odds with the needs of the customers.

The system is self-fulfilling and is often seen in larger hierarchical organisations. In order to get into a position of influence you have to play the game and so you will do what is right to win even though this may not end up being right for the customers in the long term.

Teams in organisations are set up in such a way as to reinforce team based behaviours even if they are against the objectives of the overall organisation. This is where Guerrilla Working can help. Using guerrilla like tactics to bring different people and experiences together whilst adding passion, excitement and fun can break down the barriers that have been artificially erected between should-be colleagues.

One plus one does not always equal two. Adding one drop of water to another leaves you not with two drops but a single bigger drop of water. The same is true of teams. Add two teams together effectively and you end up with a bigger team.

Showing that the walls can be breached will lead others to question their own perceptions about how teams work, or don't work together. Putting yourself and your team out by being willing to cross the inter-team divide will create a new willingness on all sides to work together. It is in these spaces that the best opportunities to create value will be found.

Enjoy your NBFs

According to the Urban Dictionary the abbreviation NBF stands for new best friend. NBF is pretty much what it says on the tin. Everyone is interesting (well nearly everyone) when you first meet them but the gloss can soon wear thin.

With Guerrilla Working you are going to make lots of NBFs and they are going to meet you. You are going to find all of them, well nearly all of them, interesting and of course they will be fascinated by your charm and enthusiasm. You'll all get on like a house on fire.

This will lead to an increase in activity with more emails, more social media and more actions to add to your ever-growing list of things to do. This shouldn't be seen as a chore but rather an inevitable consequence of getting involved. Each interaction can be seen as an opportunity to cement a new relationship with a valuable colleague or an opportunity to make a change that improves the way that the work is done. Every interaction is an opportunity to learn and to influence. Guerrilla Working can still make a difference even after you have left the theatre.

And the thing is with NBFs is that they can be here today and off to someone else tomorrow. The gloss can wear thin as the novelty rubs off. You only have one opportunity to make a first impression and you will have very few subsequent contacts in which to make or break a new relationship. Acting quickly, following up on correspondence and resolving issues will soon turn your new best friends into long term colleagues that can be relied upon to work with you to achieve your mutual aims and objectives.

Perhaps they'll even volunteer to join your band of Guerrillas.

Blog entry: Embedding

I have been thinking a lot about the relationship between the work that you do and the place that you do it and I have become more and more convinced that if place matters at all then the best location is to be as close to your customers as possible. If place doesn't matter then anywhere will do.

If someone's role is to provide support to customers then why can't they be based from that organisation's location rather then working out of our own office? It is not technology that is holding us back. If the customer has a wireless network then off we go. Even if they don't then 3G or now 4G connections are usually available, so for anyone who works through a monitor or needs to have a base out in the field, a customer's premises could offer a better alternative location than our own organisation's buildings.

It is culture that stops us. It's just not right. We can't have people sitting in customer's offices, they might ask us to do things, they might want to chat to us and ask us to solve their problems which might give them an unfair advantage over other customers. Other customers might want the same.

We need to see our people don't we? We need to know they have checked in and are beavering away on what we need them to do yet what we need them to do is to do things, chat to customers and solve their problems and make them feel valued. We want other customers to ask us for the same service.

So we tried it. We embedded a field engineer in East Durham Homes, a registered social landlord and one of our most significant clients. Rather than being based out of our Seaham office, about five miles away, they would set up shop within the customer. If there were things to do for EDH they would do them, if there weren't then they would get on with other customer issues. If they needed to visit other customers then that is what they would do. They did exactly what they would normally have done only started from the customer.

Yes, when they were in EDH people came and talked to them. People interrupted him when he was sitting at his workstation. If they didn't then he would wander around, when he could, and get involved. They asked them about how to get their ICT to work better, to fix niggling little things they would never have bothered anyone with and for general help. It was a great success. Our engineer became one of their family and helped to improve the performance of our customer and enhance our reputation.

And that is exactly what we set out to achieve. Business should not be about us winning at the expense of our customers. The success of our clients should be right up there for us. The greater their success then the greater is ours and having a very close relationship at an operational level certainly helps. As Stephen R Covey says, it is a win win situation.

The right tools

No job can be done without the right tools. All of us have tried to hammer a nail in with the heel of our shoe or undo a screw with a coin at some time and we know that it just doesn't work. You slip and take the skin off your knuckles and words come out of your mouth that would make a crow blush.

If you want to do a job properly then you need to invest some time and effort in making sure that you have everything you need to hand.

It's not as if you are travelling to Mars. You will be able to turn back to pick up something that you have forgotten and have another go at another time. Preparation is key however. Measure twice, cut once is a useful adage to remind us that planning and preparation are essential.

Having the right tools with you as you become a Guerrilla Worker could make the difference between success and failure in whatever way you have chosen to define what these are. But tools aren't always things that you can hold in your hand. Many of the tools that you need you will hold in your head or will have been prescribed by the organisation for which you work.

In this chapter I am going to describe some of the tools that you will need on your campaigns. Some belong solely to you and only you can make them work or not but others are part of the environment on which you are working and you will make a contribution to their overall success.

New technologies and ideas are being dreamt up every day and so this list of suggestions is far from extensive. You should keep one eye open on any social media streams or blogs that you follow for innovative ideas. The work place is always changing and Guerrilla Working is a great way of getting in amongst the fight, stirring things up, meeting new people, having fun and being a part of the change that you want to see. These are some of the things that you will need:

Systems and processes

I described some of the ways that I manage to Guerrilla Work in Chapter 3 and will try not to repeat them here. Only you can decide what works best for you but the aim should be to be able to work from more or less anywhere. Having support systems in place and processes that work is essential.

There are some things that you will always need, such as the ability to stay in touch with your colleagues and customers, to respond to correspondence and requests in a timely manner and to comply with any reporting requirements that your job demands.

It is a very rare person who has absolute freedom over what they can do during their working day and so you will need to be able to organise yourself effectively around the immovable boulders in your path. Time management is a prerequisite. Being always in the wrong place during work time will lead your colleagues to question your motivation and you to question whether Guerrilla Working is worthwhile.

The approach is about bringing teams of people together to create new perceptions and experiences. Reinforcing old prejudices about new ways of working is something that needs to be guarded against. You will have to be more effective, more available and even more visible than you would be in a more traditional approach as there will be sceptics waiting for you to trip up.

Make sure that you get these systems and processes in place from the start, at least the basics as they can always be refined as you go along.

Policies and procedures

Guerrilla Working relies upon trust. It is fundamental to its effective adoption. There needs to be trust between any manager and their employees that they are working productively when they are not visible. I hear it said so many times that managers like to see their employees as they can't be trusted to work properly. In truth the managers are concerned about a small number of individuals who they feel cannot be trusted but are afraid to highlight them and separate them from the greater team. Everyone ends up suffering for the sake of a small number of difficult people.

The truth is that even if you can see someone there is no guarantee that they are working effectively or productively. Their mind may be wandering, they might be concentrating on something inappropriate or they may be deliberately avoiding work. They would have to be monitored at all times to be certain that work was being done and this would be counterproductive as well as very costly.

Yet I've never met an organisation without some people of concern. If we could start today and hand pick the best people available after a while we would end up with one or two problem individuals. That is because people and circumstances change. They fall ill, they become distracted, they have things on their mind and they have problems outside work which impinge upon their performance. Sometimes people just don't fit into the culture of an organisation or the systems that it employs. As Professor John Seddon, Managing Director of Vanguard Consulting says 'It's not the people, it's the system'.

So it makes no sense to hold back on the potential productivity and cultural improvements possible through Guerrilla Working for the sake of a couple of renegades. One of the first managers that I reported to advised me not to be unduly concerned about complaints. 'If you have no complaints then you are not trading' he said to me at my interview and to a degree he is right. So if you don't have some problem employees then either you aren't employing anyone, you are deluding yourself or you just haven't discovered them yet.

Trust also goes the other way. For Guerrilla Working to be effective then the employees must trust that their manager is looking out for them and that they have confidence in how they are performing. Working without the protective blanket of a traditional office environment can be unnerving.

So both managers have to trust and employees have to trust. The organisation has to be grounded in trust.

Managers and employees need to have at their disposal a set of guiding principles which allow them to trust the people who work for them in order that everyone is clear about what is permissible and what is not. These should include the obvious things such as what work they are expected to do, how many hours, in what format, how it will be delivered etc. There are many other things that need to be considered however such as the hours in which work is permitted; how to keep in touch; how often an employee is expected to attend meetings and; how to report sickness absence.

It could be that people would like to work late in the evening or through the night but this may not fit in with the needs of the business. Contact with customers or colleagues may be an essential requirement of the role and so would not be appropriate. So called unsocial-hours working is a common request for homeworkers processing Revenues and Benefits payments in local government yet the complex systems that underpin their work need down time to process and back up data and so there are times that certain types of work cannot be done. These need to be defined.

Requests for different working patterns can often reflect the lifestyle needs of the employee. Childcare or other caring needs could lead to the request for staggered shifts with work being done in three or four shorter working periods in the day to accommodate school runs for example. How will it be clear that someone is at work and someone is not? How long or how short can a working period be? These need to be considered in any policy or procedure. It also needs to be clear that no one can work and look after someone at the same time.

Different working patterns may be required to accommodate more than one employment. By the end of 2012, the number of people in part-time employment in the UK had risen to 8.13million[39] or 27% of the total number of people in work. Of these, 1.4million had taken part-time as they could not find full-time work.

In recent years there has been a noticeable increase in so-called 'zero-hours' contracts[40], where people agree to be available for work as and when required but have no guaranteed hours or times of work. This has been in response to the difficult economic conditions of the first decade of the 21st century as employers try to find cost-effective ways of meeting short-term staffing needs by creating a pool of people who can be called upon to match the demands of the business.

Estimates of the numbers of people working to such contracts vary but the Chartered Institute of Personnel and Development put the number in the UK at around one million by the end of 2013. A survey[41] showed that many workers are happy with the flexibility and low level of commitment that zero-hours contracts bring yet just under half of the sample said that they would like more hours.

Many people now have more than on job to contend with. A quarter of working mothers have more than one and 15% have more than two[42].

---

[39] Office for National Statistics August 2012
[40] ACAS
[41] http://www.cipd.co.uk/pressoffice/press-releases/cipd-research-zero-hours-contracts-unfairly-demonised-oversimplified-261113.aspx
[42] www.workingmums.co.uk

Policies and procedures must reflect these and other emerging modern working-practices and address the question of whether or not they are acceptable to the organisation.

Consideration also needs to be given to those groups of people who are unable to pick and choose their place or hours of work such as machine operators or reception staff. It needs to be clear in any statement of terms and conditions the degree of flexibility that is allowed and this needs to be based upon practicalities rather then perceptions and tradition.

We need to question our assumptions about place. Does that role really require the person to work in that specific office at those specific times? Why can't a call centre operator for example be placed in amongst their customers rather than in a separate team? Can the machine be moved to go with the operator? Do the processes we employ reflect the demands that are placed upon the business by the customers?

And then there are those people who like to come to work for the sense of belonging and camaraderie that they get from working with their colleagues. A friend of mine who was retiring from the Police said to me that the thing he would miss most about the job was the bonds that he had built with his colleagues over the years, especially on the night shift. The sense of working together to achieve something or even just being together as part of something is a strong human requirement.

Guerrilla Working does not break teams, it builds them. Remember it is the deliberate mixing up of people and teams, bringing talent together wherever it matters to solve issues and create opportunities. It is about breaking down the perceptions of what work is and reforming it around the needs of the organisation, its people and, most importantly, its customers.

Policies and procedures must support these objectives. They need to be enablers rather than inhibiters yet they are often written from a risk averse position, that is to protect the organisation rather than to enhance it. Of course policies must consider the 'what if', what would we do if this happened but Guerrilla Working policies must ask what if we let go?

Using technology

Of course technology is going to be a great help. In the land of technology the person with the extension lead is king. (When you are out and about the first rule is to steal electricity. Make sure you always charge your laptop or phone when you can. You never know how long you are going to be away from civilisation.)

Much of our ability to work in different and more agile ways has come on the back of technology. Portable devices such as laptops, tablets and smartphones have opened up all sorts of places as suitable for work and the proliferation of public wireless networks and mobile connections means that being online is very often a possibility.

If your work requires you to be about and about, if you are always on the move then having access to somewhere where you can connect to your systems in a secure way, to make use of that spare hour that you have between appointments can make the difference between being on top or chasing your tail. But don't worry, office space is available in every sizable town. Just grab your laptop or tablet and head for the many cafes and high street stores that offer free wireless access. For the price of a cup of tea you can get a lot done.

Yet technology need not be restricted to Information and Communication Technology. Not everything needs to end up as high-tech. The advent of precision cutting and three-dimensional printing is going to create new ways of addressing work. Projects such as OpenDesk[43] and FabHub[44] are changing the way that furniture and other everyday items are created and used.

---

[43] https://www.opendesk.cc/
[44] https://www.fabhub.io/

OpenDesk unites furniture buyers with a network of local makers who are able to make bespoke pieces available with varying degrees of completion including plans, flat pack, ready to assemble and fully assembled units. Office furniture will soon become portable and allow people to set up shop when and wherever it is needed.

Who knows what the future has in store for us? Predictions are often wildly inaccurate. The future has always been about technology, hasn't it? In the future we were going to have robots that will do all the work, driverless cars that fly, jet packs and silver high tech clothing. We won't be sitting down to eat but instead have some pills that give us all the energy and nutrients that we need.

Yet the future hasn't turned out like that. We are always living in someone's future but we're still going to work, our cars are firmly on the ground and I'm looking forward to pie and mash. So how come we get predictions so wrong? How come our lives aren't like the Jetsons[45] or Ed Straker from UFO[46]?

Because life isn't about technology, it is about people. The revolution that we are witnessing right now may seem like a digital technology one but in fact it is a human revolution. The most successful digital technologies are those that improve the interaction between humans. The mobile phone was life changing as it allowed people to connect from wherever they were. The picture phone was a great invention not because it took photos but because we could share them with our colleagues. The smartphone is impressive because it allows us to have a wealth of information at our fingertips and empowers us to connect with others in ways that were just not possible a few years ago.

Technology is unimportant until people find its use and adapt their lifestyle to accommodate the opportunity that it presents. The same needs to be true of you. The most important technology that you carry

[45] http://en.wikipedia.org/wiki/The_Jetsons
[46] http://en.wikipedia.org/wiki/UFO_(TV_series)

with you will be that that works for you and fits in with the way that you want to work.

Pen and paper are not the most modern of broadcast media but they have worked for centuries and are difficult to supersede in many circumstances. I used to carry with me a day book (an A4 pad but it sounds better) and a range of pens but now my laptop and smartphone do for me.

I keep in touch using a multi-media approach. I described this in chapter 6 and so won't go through it all again. I use email a lot. I know it is not so fashionable these days but it has some advantages over other communications tools. The most important for me is that it is easy to record and save. It is also easy to maintain as a conversation thread and it is a format that nearly everyone understands. I can also write emails at a time that is convenient for me and send them at a time which is convenient for the recipient.

I'm ruthless with my inbox however. I get palpitations when it gets over fifty (it's at fourteen as I write this). I deal with the majority of my mail as it comes in when it is not rude to do so. Most can be actioned very quickly anyway through either a quick yes, thanks or by deleting it or forwarding it. Letting it build up is when it becomes a problem.

I save all the attachments and mails that I need in my home folders (not Outlook folders) and restrict myself to less than 500 MB of email storage space. This is a quarter of the space that I am 'entitled' too due to my position but for me it is a good discipline.

I also use rules to split out and divert some mail into other folders. All mail copied to me goes straight into a 'CC' folder on the assumption that if it is important then I would have been sent it rather than copied. I get round to that when I have time and this saves me from the hell that comes from copying the world.

I've never really understood why email has such a bad reputation these days but it is probably because of the amount of spam and junk going round. These can be filtered out easily though. I do worry that people use their email as evidence of something that was agreed or not and that they store it away just in case they find they need to defend their position at some time in the future.

Social media plays a big role in the way I do my job as well. It is a great way of capturing the mood of the people you work with and to let everyone know, in a general way, what you are up to. Using social media opens you up to scrutiny. It increases the perception of you as a person and shows that you are available. There are so many applications to choose from now and, no doubt there will be more coming along tomorrow.

One of the technology tools I really like to use is online chat. I use Microsoft's Lync but there are many others. I use it as part of our limited, but developing, Unified Communications (UC) approach. For the uninitiated UC is the integration of real-time communication services such as instant messaging (sometimes known as chat), presence information, telephony, video conferencing and data sharing. It is not necessarily a single system but rather a common approach.

For me it offers two main advantages. The first is that I can show my status. Once I am logged in I can show to everyone else who is also logged in whether I am available, in a meeting, not to be disturbed, back in five minutes and so on. At a glance I can see if someone I would like to communicate with is available. Of course I can check their diaries but this would take a little longer.

I find this particularly useful when dealing with customer problems. Rather than chasing down an individual I can check who is available from that team and make contact.

The second advantage is the chat itself. Using instant messaging I can enter into a conversation that is in real-time but does not rely on real-time. Instant messaging is a misnomer in that its beauty is that you can hold a conversation over a protracted length of time. I can open up multiple conversations and chat away. My colleagues can respond as and when they are available. If they need to take a phone call during our chat it is no problem. They can simply pick up the thread again once they have finished. I can even leave my desktop for several hours and come back to the topic. It's like when you meet an old friend after many years and you pick up the conversation where you left off.

Chat has a different level of language than the more formal channels. It allows you to be far more familiar and the addition of emoticons, little cartoon-like images, help by adding an emotional context, a smiley when you are feeling good or an angry face when you want to convey frustration. Chat allows you to combine the direct interaction of email with the familiarity of social media and allows you to stay in touch wherever you are, as long as you are connected.

There is no substitute however for face to face contact for the most important of conversations and interactions. That is the way that humans operate. Technology is fine in that allows us to communicate instantaneously and over great distances yet real communication requires all of our senses. Ideally we need to pick up on the nuance of body language and tone and these are difficult to detect once digitally transcribed.

I suspect that smell or other chemical impulses play an important role. For example, research has shown that making a fearful expression, like opening the eyes very wide, leads us to breathe in deeply through our noses, enhances our perception, and accelerates our eye movements. This in turn allows us to spot potentially dangerous targets quickly. Disgust reactions, known as sensory rejection, warn others to avoid potentially noxious chemical by lowering our eyebrows and wrinkling our noses.[47]

Studies in Utrecht University have shown that emotional changes can be transferred form one person to another and across gender using sweat

---

[47] http://www.redorbit.com/news/science/1112726427/emotional-communication-uses-nose-110612/

even when the originator is not present. Their findings provide support for the embodied social-communication model, suggesting that chemical signals act as a medium through which people can be emotionally synchronized outside of conscious awareness[48].

Technology has so far not addressed these aspects of communication though proposals exist to develop a wearable device, which can stimulate smell and taste senses to communicate remotely.[49] It can only be a matter of time.

So technology can really support our efforts to improve our approach to work. Remember that the purpose Guerrilla Working is to uncover talent, increase visibility, create new realities, provoke ideas and to have fun. Technology allows us to pull off the magic trick of being able to have face to face contact when it is most useful, that is in building relationships and using all of our sensory communications while at the same time remaining in contact with the rest of our social networks.

Technology sets us free from the shackles of a fixed work location and allows us to work where we can be at our most effective.

Staying safe

As a Guerrilla Worker you will find yourself working at times in unfamiliar places and meeting people that you do not know. You will not be found in your usual spot and your existing work colleagues may be used to not seeing you for days on end. You might not be missed.

So who is looking out for you? Who will have your back when you are not around? Who will have your interest at heart and make sure that you are alive and well? We've talked at length about communication and keeping in touch remotely but is there someone in your team who would notice if you hadn't been in contact for some time?

---

[48] http://www.psychologicalscience.org/index.php/news/releases/the-knowing-nose-chemosignals-communicate-human-emotions.html
[49] http://mixedrealitylab.org/projects/all-projects/digital-smell-and-taste-communication/

A friend of mine once asked me if I could be his wingman. At first I hadn't got a clue what he meant and so I did what we always do these days when we don't know something, I looked it up on the internet. I referred to this already in chapter 6 in that the job of the wingman is to watch the back of the lead pilot.

The idea of my friend was not flying related but rather that each of us would support the other by promoting our activities, bringing each other up in conversations and generally looking out for each other. I think his notion of a wingman used to be known as a friend but perhaps a little more focussed in its intention.

We all need a wingman, someone who will look out for us and is aware if we haven't been seen around for a while. We all need someone who has our welfare at heart especially if you are not going to have a regular work pattern.

On a practical level there are some things that you should know about the places in which you are working, things that may be very useful in an emergency such as fire exits or where you can get something to eat.

Every time we get on a flight we have to sit through the pre-flight safety demonstration. They are required by the basic international air safety standards set by the International Civil Aviation Organization and national civil aviation authorities. Most of us will try to stay focussed while the attendants point out the exits and the oxygen masks but we've seen it all before. Several airlines have tried to make the demonstrations more interesting and the use of video has helped. Many can be found on YouTube and the Virgin America one is worth checking out.[50]

The chances of being involved in an airplane incident where you will need to remember the safety instructions are thankfully rare but if it happens you'll be glad that you hadn't been reading the paper as the plane taxied towards the runway.

---

[50] http://www.youtube.com/watch?v=DtyfiPlHsIg

All hotel rooms show the fire exits and the route you should take to escape from the building on the back of the door. Train carriages now show similar information in the vestibules at the end of each coach and they are worth a check just in case.

Find out how to get out, where the fire exits are, where the toilets are and the best places to eat.

But it's not just your personal safety you should be aware of. We've seen that Guerrilla Working is enhanced by technology and the internet can be a dangerous place. It represents the whole gamut of human society with all its good and bad characters. There are the more unscrupulous types who are looking to hack into your computer for their own purposes. Basic standards of computer security such as anti-virus and encryption should be adopted.

You should also be careful about the information that you are carrying with you. What would happen if you were to lose it by leaving it in an office or a train? If we were carrying a briefcase containing £100k you would be very careful about where you left it. You'd probably keep your hands on it at all times. Yet the value of the information that you carry around with you could well be worth much more.

The Information Commissioner's Office (ICO)[51] issued fines of more than £4 million in 2013 for breaches of the Data Protection Act, with the highest fines being for the loss of sensitive personal data. Financial penalties not to mention the loss of reputation are to be considered. You should only carry information that you would be prepared to lose. Everything else should be encrypted or held on remote storage.

You shouldn't leave any confidential information lying around in your office (it is amazing how many people do) and you certainly shouldn't leave it lying around in someone else's. If in doubt the best advice is don't carry it with you.

---

[51] http://www.ico.org.uk/

Get some head space

As a Guerrilla Worker you can work anywhere and at any time. You can fit in with the needs of your customers or the needs of your team but don't forget about your own needs. Just because you can doesn't mean you have to. There is a temptation to work at all times and if you are not careful that's just what will happen. You'll end of working at work and working from home. Some discipline is required to make sure you always retain some time to unwind.

Life shouldn't be all about work, indeed work shouldn't be all about work. In my book it is perfectly acceptable to pepper the things you must do with things that you enjoy doing. Go on, treat yourself at regular intervals.

Research since the early sixties has shown evidence for the existence of ultradian activity cycles lasting between 80 – 100 minutes that occur between wakefulness and sleep. Kleitman[52] proposed a Basic rest Activity Cycle model (BRAC) which has been generally accepted and suggested that there are four different cyclical processes at play, including physiological and psychological, related to: alertness; performance; body fluid and electrolyte balance and; gastric motility.

Accordingly human performance can be maximised thorough bursts of activity lasting around 90 minutes interspersed with a break of 20 minutes or so. The traditional day split into three eight hour segments of work, rest and play is a myth. Think about it, our work is much easier if it is broken down into more manageable chunks with something to distract us in-between. Hunt a little and rest. Gather a little and rest. Socialise a little and rest. After all, a change is as good as a rest.

A Guerrilla Worker needs to be mindful of him or herself. By all means fill your day but make sure there is time to fill bits with your own interests and there is time for you to clear your head, to get some head space.

---

[52] http://link.springer.com/chapter/10.1007/978-1-4471-1969-2_13#page-1

I've put this in a chapter on 'The Right Tools' and you may be asking what tools are involved. I did start the chapter by saying that tools aren't always things that you can hold in your hand. Many of the tools that you need you will hold in your head. A bad worker blames his tools but a good worker makes sure that his tools are well looked after. A Guerrilla Worker needs to look after their best tools.

And there are tools available to give you the head space that you need. Everyone should find their own approach to relaxation but I was encouraged by some friends to try meditation. I was interested whether this could help me to unravel some of my hectic noise inside my head and ended up reading a book by Andy Puddicombe called 'Get some Headspace'[53]. As a complete novice to the subject, this book was worth the read.

Andy Puddicombe is a registered clinical meditation consultant who practices and teaches meditation and uses it in his clinic. A former Buddhist monk, he has travelled all over the world and has now set up Headspace in the UK to demystify meditation and make it accessible and relevant to as many people as possible.

His book took me through the many benefits of meditation and also mindfulness, which is being self-aware and able to live 'in the moment'. It introduces the concept of 'headspace', the ability to create space in your own head that allows you to see your own life more clearly. This is done through a ten minute a day meditation session referred to as Take 10.

There are 10 exercises to show you the different ways that you can get started and 10 suggestions as to why living life more mindfully is worth pursuing:

- Perspective – choosing how you see your life
- Communication – relating to others
- Appreciation – smelling the roses

---

[53] http://www.getsomeheadspace.com/

- Kindness – towards both yourself and others
- Compassion – in the shoes of others
- Balance – a sense of equanimity
- Acceptance – resistance is futile
- Composure – letting go of impatience
- Dedication – sticking with it
- Presence – living life skilfully.

The book ends with some stories of people who came to the clinic and that have helped themselves through meditation.

When I read the book I felt a bit let down at first but after trying some of the exercises I began to feel the benefit and changed my view. If you already want to try meditation but haven't found a way to get started then this I would recommend this as a place to start.

Taking time out every day, even if it's only for ten minutes certainly helps me to cope with the majority of the things that working life can throw at me. It may seem counterintuitive but doing less can lead to being able to do more. What works for me may not be right for everyone and so it is important to invest some time in finding what works for you because at the end of the day you are the most important tool in your box.

The loneliness of a Guerrilla Worker

It is worth mentioning at this point that being a Guerrilla Worker is not always going to be easy. You're away from your normal routine, away from your support structures and well out of your comfort zone. Even the most ardent of devotee will struggle from time to time to keep to the cause.

Even though Guerrilla Working is about bringing people together in new ways, creating new perceptions and new relationships it can still be a lonely place. Some of the loneliest people live in the busiest cities and we mustn't confuse friends with acquaintances.

There is no shame in admitting that you need a break and to make you way back to the fold where the coffee is always on and the natives are friendly. For many going to work is an opportunity to spend time with their friends and colleagues. Belonging is a natural human need.

In a very unscientific survey of the people in one of the buildings we operate from, we asked the question: 'If you could work from anywhere within the organisation, including home, would you still base yourself from this building?' Of those that expressed a preference there was a majority who would opt for the status quo. Most of the respondents, given the choice, would still like to come to work in the same way and to the same place as they do today.

The reasons given were primarily to do with companionship and camaraderie. The banter was good and they would miss the team interaction. Yet we must not confuse being based and working. My base is County Hall and I used to have an office at my disposal on the fifth floor. Some weeks however I spent as little as two hours there which is one of the reasons it is now used as a meeting room.

As it happens, the people who are based out of the building surveyed are already very mobile. They spend a lot of time with customers or fixing problems due to the extended nature of our business. I come across them in lots of different places. As the Frank Sinatra song goes though:

'It's oh, so nice to go trav'ling,
But it's so much nicer
Yes, it's so much nicer to come home.'

Guerrilla Working is not about getting up early to bag the best desks in an open plan office. It is not about removing all notions of team structures across an organisation. It is about working in the best place that the job dictates. It is about getting in amongst the teams that you rely on or serve and developing new relations and structures. It is about working where the value is created.

There is value in belonging. There is value in team building, sharing information, developing working practices and swapping stories. Being a Guerrilla Worker does not exclude you from these things. Indeed it should be recognised that such attachments are fundamentally human and need to be built into our routines. Sometimes you just need to go back home and recharge your batteries.

Using stories

There is nothing more human than a story. Using stories is a great way of breaking down barriers, of getting people to engage with you and to get your point to stick. I've used stories throughout this book.

Stories have been used since time immemorial. Our stories are who we are. They can be a very powerful tool in getting your message across in a way that will resonate with your listener.

After nourishment, shelter and companionship, stories are the thing we need most in the world.[54]

There are some stories that are innate. They are built into our genetic code, stories that we all knew before we were ever told them. There are stories that we have heard many times but we feel that we have known them all along. Just as a bird knows how to build a nest or a silkworm knows how to cast its cocoon there bits of information that are locked deep inside ourselves that are unlocked by stories.

We know them already, stories of a virgin birth or of a great flood, tales of a god sent down to live amongst the mortals or a mythical fire-breathing creature or a sword with mystical powers and fables about a poisoned apple or the wicked step mother.

They are stories of vengeance and destruction, hope and forgiveness, suffering and survival, gods and daemons. They are the background to human existence, a narrative that explains who we are, how we got here and how we manage the great struggle of living in a world that has

---

[54] http://www.goodreads.com/author/show/3618.Philip_Pullman

always been beyond our comprehension.

Stories are told around the world by many cultures and in many guises. They are adopted and adapted, transcribed into words and moving images, set to music and dance, retold over and over again. Stories are fundamental to who we are because they are the easiest way to remember something. If you want to get your message across, tell it as a story.

If history were taught in the form of stories, it would never be forgotten.[55]

I use stories at work to set the tone, to highlight the positive things that we achieve and to encourage cooperation and integration across the various teams. We use positive stories to open up all of our management meetings. They create a much more upbeat atmosphere than by focusing on the things that go wrong. Telling stories about things that go wrong are easy and telling them about things that go right takes more effort.

They pay dividend though and it is worth just thinking that few minutes longer about the message you want to get across and putting it into a story format to make it more sticky. The same goes for presentations. No one likes to see PowerPoint slides filled with words while someone goes through them line by line, especially when the presenter is facing the screen. Most of us can read and so what's the point of taking us through them? If we can't read then what's the point of the words.

Stop doing presentations and start telling stories. Replace as many words as you can with pictures. Your audience will remember the narrative through association with the picture and thank you for not doing another tedious presentation. If you struggle with this then have a go at PechaKucha[56], a presentation format devised by Astrid Klein and Mark Dytham of Klein Dytham Architecture. It is a simple concept,

---

[55] http://en.wikipedia.org/wiki/Rudyard_Kipling
[56] http://www.pechakucha.org/

highly effective and great fun. The speaker is limited to 20 images and each is shown for 20 seconds only. They are timed and so there is no hanging about. I have been told that words are not allowed but I'm not sure this is the case. They are of little use anyway, you simply don't have time to go through them.

Whilst telling stories is one of the most natural things that we can do it can be difficult to weave them into your work. They can seem contrived and awkward. All skills and talents need to be nurtured and developed and fortunately there are many organisations that are willing to help. Typing 'using stories in business' into your favourite search engine will bring up over a billion related articles and so it is strange that it is not a more widely used technique. They are used all the time though, when we are chatting with people in the corridor and over the water-cooler but it is their use in a more formal context that requires help.

OnBrand Partners[57] has a series of modules in their TakeON! programme that encourage conversation and storytelling. Engaging teams in dialogue and conversation is much more effective than the download style of communication that is most prevalent in business. Stories can be used to break down opinions, urban myths and common beliefs that bind teams together. Capturing real and positive stories about your own operation can help to build a new set of cultural standards.

Sogno[58] use drama based coaching to create new perspectives and leave our old, ineffective behaviours behind. Sometimes to see who we really are we have to become somebody else and setting up scenarios in which we could replay out stories, both good and bad, allow us to rethink our approach to each other and our customers.

The point isn't really that other people can help you but rather that you

---

[57] http://www.onbrandpartners.com/
[58] http://www.sognoltd.com/index.php

make the effort to see yourself from a different perspective. Guerrilla Working is about mixing working locations and styles to create new relationships and new perspectives. Learning to relay these experiences using stories brings them into the vernacular and part of your new culture.

Leo Tolstoy, one of the world's greatest authors, moral thinkers and social reformers wrote that 'All great literature is one of two stories; a man goes on a journey or a stranger comes to town.'

Guerrilla Working is one of those great stories. You go on a journey or a stranger appears within your team.

To hell with facts! We need stories![59]

---

[59] http://www.goodreads.com/author/show/7285.Ken_Kesey

Blog entry: In the future

The future is going to be different. I don't mean we'll be living under water or wearing some weird clothing. Styles will change and things will come in and out of vogue. Indeed you know you're getting old when you come back into fashion.

No, the future will be different for one reason and that is we will all have access to huge amounts of information and data. We think there is a lot now but it's growing at an exponential rate. Computing power will keep up. Moore's law will see to that.

In the future new products will be data products and new services will be information services.

To live in the future we will need new skills. It won't be enough to know things. There will just be too much for anyone to know. The greatest skills required will be how to find information and how to assemble new ideas into products or services that add value. This could be financial value, social value or informational value. You can decide.

In the future data will be free. Information will be the ether that flows around us. Value will be created by using the data rather than possessing it.

Ideas will be created by people coming together. Innovation will form at the clash between experiences and cultures. Old rules will be challenged, guards replaced and life will be very different.

Paradigms lost.

In the future organisations won't respect the physical boundaries in which they were born. They won't be bricks and mortar, glass and steel. They will be castles of thought, traded markets of ideation, agglomeration of concepts. Future workers will align themselves to outcomes. They will be paid by values. Sectors won't compete but will work together to create true social innovation.

But we'll still need adventurers, those who dare to look elsewhere, search out new opportunities and go beyond the fringes of the known world. We'll need people who aren't afraid to mix it up with other tribes, other cultures and bring new ideas and experiences together. We'll need go-betweens, translators and interpreters, those who can transfer ideas onto white boards, story tellers, integrators, visualizers, realists, pragmatists, pessimists and optimists.

Above all we will need people who want to look for another way. We will need Guerrilla Workers.

Summary

By now you should be itching to get on with it and to become a Guerrilla Worker. This chapter is about just that. It is a summary of the things I have already covered.

When I think about the work that I have been involved in over the last thirty years, simply but not simplistically, there is work that can only be done in and amongst my team, there is work that can only be done in and amongst my customers and there is work that can be done anywhere. Guerrilla Working allows me to address these different types of work and allows me to be wherever I can maximise the impact that I make.

If you need to be with your team then make sure that you are all together doing what you do. If you need to be with your customers then why not sit alongside them and if your work can be done anywhere then anywhere will do. Guerrilla Working enables you to make the greatest use of the most important asset that you have – yourself and ensures that you maximise your impact.

Guerrilla Working isn't difficult but changing the way that you work is hard. It is not physically or technologically challenging yet it requires an enormous cultural change and it has to start with you.

Gandhi's often quoted 'Be the change that you wish to see in the world' says it all. Be the person that you want to be, work in the places that will make the most impact and become a Guerrilla Worker. Good luck!

Benefits of Guerrilla Working

We have covered these in the previous chapters but it is worth bringing them together:

Change

- It is a challenge to all of the procedures, practices and tenets that hold current organisations together but are in fact holding them back.
- It will encourage teams to break out of preconceived patterns of work, the way they have always been done around here and to reflect on possible alternatives.
- Truly flexible individual and group working is possible and sustainable by breaking down barriers and improving communications and understanding.
- It breaks the link between where you work and what you do and allows work activities to take place where the action is, where value is created.
- The separation of the management of people and the delivery of task is enabled and acts as a provocation allowing people to see things in a new light.
- It create new realities, provoke ideas and adds excitement to the business.
- It is fun.

Talent

- It uncovers talent that you already have and is an effective way of binding people to the organisation in which they work.
- It brings talent together wherever it matters to solve issues and create opportunities that exist within the place of work.

- It creates a clear idea of who does what, who leads in which area and who the movers and shakers are.
- And of course it also does the reverse by increasing your visibility by showing others who you are.

Develop

- It allows managers to focus on working to develop the skills of their colleagues while ensuring that they broaden their experience.
- It allows people to meet people they already know but in new ways. It allows them to build relationships in the most human of ways through face to face contact.
- It creates new opportunities for people to get involved in areas of a business that they may not be used to. They get to play with new toys, meet new people, bring different perceptions and rise to new challenges.
- It maximises face to face time with a wide audience while maintaining a good communications mix.
- It allows organisations to create a single brand that supports its overall objectives.

Knowledge

- It allows individuals to reach out to colleagues and customers in a way that shared experiences can be created.
- It allows us to experience work practices and ideas in practice before considering them in theory.
- It lays down new knowledge that can be used in addressing future challenges.
- It gives rise to many good stories from the people you meet and the places that you go which can be used to fight the good fight.

Considerations and bear traps

Guerrilla Working is liberating. It can change the relationship that you have with your work and create new ways for you to engage with your colleagues and customers and understand your mutual business. But it requires a cultural change and changing a culture is difficult. It requires a groundswell of change. It needs leaders and it needs first followers. A fish rots from the head down as they say. To change the way things are requires people with vision and determination to make a difference.

Being a Guerrilla Worker yourself is within your own gift yet the real benefit comes with the spread of the approach across the wider organisation. Everything new looks odd at first and hindsight eventually makes it right. To be different requires individuals who dare to be different and it requires others who can see the possibilities and dare to join in.

Derek Sivers sums it up very simply in his inspirational video short 'Leadership Lessons from Dancing Guy.'[60] A leader needs the guts to stand alone and look ridiculous. But what he's doing is so simple, it's almost instructional. This is key. You must be easy to follow! It takes guts to be a first follower! You stand out and brave ridicule, yourself. Being a first follower is an under-appreciated form of leadership. The first follower transforms a lone nut into a leader. If the leader is the flint, the first follower is the spark that makes the fire.

Guerrilla Working is simple to follow, it doesn't need particularly specialist equipment but it needs lone nuts to ridicule themselves and most importantly first followers to turn it into a movement. So when you see someone following the ideals of Guerrilla Working then you should encourage them and support them though their journey as much as you can.

Leaders don't need to be at the top of an organisation however, they can be peppered throughout. People more often look to their immediate colleagues and supervisors for inspiration rather than the lofty and inaccessible heights of senior management. Managers can

---

[60] Leadership Lessons from Dancing Guy

learn from their teams and those who are in the position to lead can learn from those who report to them. The quality of a good leader lies in the ability to learn and adapt to new opportunities. Sometimes we need to lead from behind.

It helps if senior management are supportive though. Organisations transform more quickly if it is led from the 'top'. Leaders who hang onto the trappings of office power, the capacious office, the expansive hardwood desk and the named parking space set the tone and constantly remind employees that this is the accepted way. If you don't think it should be then you need to make the break and take every opportunity to remind those with influence that what they are doing is reinforcing old and outdated working practices.

There is a lot of talk about modern and agile ways of working yet people listen with their eyes as well as their ears and if what they see doesn't match with what comes out of your mouth then you will lose the chance to influence. You need to start with yourself, encourage your followers and take every opportunity to expose gently the foibles of those who are not yet on-board.

Remember this is a battle. You are fighting the practices built up over centuries of industrialisation. There is a lot of emotional capital tied up in the way that organisations have been built. People get to the top by playing the system and if it was good enough to get them there why should they change their ways now? Because work is changing that is why. What we have done in the past will not be good enough for the future.

Slavery and feudalism are no longer accepted yet they still exist and it took people who were brave enough to say these things were wrong to change the norm. My home town is the birth place of the suffragette Emily Wilding Davison. A hundred years ago she ran in front of the King's horse 'Anmer' during the Epsom Derby with the intention of placing a sash in support of the suffragette movement around its neck. You will have seen the old footage showing the horse colliding with

Emily who broke her skull and died four days later in Epsom Cottage Hospital.

Apparently she was not fighting for votes for all women, just equality with men. At the start of the twentieth century only around thirty per cent of men could vote yet today we enjoy universal suffrage in this country. I'm not suggesting that anyone should lay down their life, intentionally or not for something they so strongly believe in but it highlights the catalytic nature of individual actions.

You will need to have a lot of stamina because Guerrilla Working goes against many of the 'ways that things are done around her.' Circumstances will go against you and you will be constantly trying to avoid the bear traps laid intentionally or unintentionally before you. Most people like to belong and understand structures and hierarchies. Those in authority have managed to claw their way through them and turkeys don't vote for Christmas.

Persuading people to change the way that they work is asking them to take themselves out of their comfort zones. It is asking them to be more visible, to find what the reality actually is and to question their own role and position. Many fear raising their heads above the parapet for fear of being shot. In many instances the best thing to do is to do nothing and just go along with the flow.

Most organisations, especially those that are long established, have developed survival mechanisms. They automatically now what do to if they are attacked or injured and have unwritten procedures in place to counter change. It is like dark matter. You can feel it but you can't see it. It's a weak force but with a long reach. You need to fight it but it is hard because the dark matter is the essence of the organisation, the culture, the unwritten code by which it operates which everyone understands but no one knows, never documented and never codified.

Many have tried to question it, tried to beat it and many have failed but they were not Guerrilla Workers.

Building trust

The fundamental issue that underpins all Guerrilla Working is trust. For it to be effective there must be trust between all parties, managers, supervisors, workers, customers and suppliers. You also need to trust yourself and your judgment.

To achieve such trust two things must happen: A clear understanding of the aims and objectives of either parties or organisations and; a set of ground rules that allow workers the freedom to operate as they see best while working to achieve these aims and objectives.

If an organisation wants to break away from a command and control approach that relies heavily on a hierarchical decision making structure then the core values and an understanding of its objectives must flow throughout like a name in a stick of rock. Having a common set of objectives is difficult however, especially in a complex environment. There is a tendency to oversimplify by boiling the business down into a set of meaningless values and outcomes that become motherhood and apple pie.

What results is a bland mission statement that talks about being number one in the market, adding shareholder value or providing the best customer service. Whilst these are all well and good they are difficult to translate into action.

Everyone needs to relate the work that they are engaged in to the greater good of the overall business and the needs of its customers. Workers need to be able to understand simply that their work fits into the general direction of the business.

There is a story about a systems supplier who was presenting an application to a manager at Toyota (again) who stopped him and asked 'How will this software help me to sell more cars?' The salesman replied that he didn't know whether it would at which point the manager politely advised him that, in that case he would not be interested.

A balance needs to be struck between the ability to remember and comprehend against the wide variety of tasks and functions that you are engaged in. They will need to be believable as well. The communication and marketing of values and objectives will need to be made repeatedly and often.

In Durham County Council's ICT strategy we have tried to capture our purpose in three sentences. Everything always happens in threes and it seems that people find this an easy number to remember.

- To provide a secure, stable and robust environment which enables Durham County Council to utilise existing hardware and software applications as effectively and efficiently as is practical.
- To work with Members, Service Groupings, Residents, Partners, Learners and other interested parties to develop or implement ICT solutions to help meet their objectives.
- To identify new ICT opportunities and provide technical expertise to enable Durham County Council to deliver services in a new way, whilst improving efficiency, reducing operational costs or increase income.

To paraphrase though our purpose is:

- To keep things running.
- To help the delivery services to move the business forward.
- To provide the technical expertise.

Our number one activity must be to ensure that the underlying systems that allow the delivery services to do whatever they come in to do are available and running effectively. Without these there is no opportunity to add the higher value added services. Without strong foundations there is no point in building the walls. Productive time is a concept that we must keep in our thoughts. Any loss in ICT systems leads to a drop in productivity. Our job may not be to make cars but it is to provide services and an application that isn't running won't help us to achieve any objectives at all.

These short statements hide a multitude of sins however as the annual services plan can include more than a hundred specific objectives.

To try and make our business easier to comprehend we repeat that we do five things: Maintain; Fix; Supply; Change and; Inform.

You can imagine the analogy of having a car. We take it into the garage periodically to have it serviced which is maintenance. We do this to avoid it breaking down but from time to time this happens and then it will need to be fixed. We may need some new accessories such as a roof rack and that fits into supply while when we come to think about a new car we might want to know about miles per gallon or boot capacity and this counts as inform and then change.

Our customers think of us mostly in terms of fix. Just like electricity, ICT is something that goes on in the background and often only comes to the fore when it is not available. Yet we do so much more and the added value activities (change and inform) are the most important in the long run for the business and so a constant campaign is required to keep the message fresh.

Analogies help us to get our heads around our business in conceptual terms. There has been a lot of discussion as to whether what we call the things that we do are accurate or fairly represent the complexity of our business and alternative words suggested. We will build these into our refresh of the ICT strategy but the most important thing is that the team is able to take time out to think about what we are here to deliver.

Perhaps we need to work harder to reduce our mission and objectives into a single sentence.

Google's mission is to organise the world's information and make it universally accessible and useful.

Patagonia is a business that makes clothes for climbing, skiing, snowboarding, surfing, fly fishing, paddling and trail running. Their reason for being is to 'Build the best product, cause no unnecessary harm, use business to inspire and implement solutions to the environmental crisis.'

'For us at Patagonia, a love of wild and beautiful places demands participation in the fight to save them, and to help reverse the steep decline in the overall environmental health of our planet. We donate our time, services and at least 1% of our sales to hundreds of grassroots environmental groups all over the world who work to help reverse the tide.'

Blake Mycoskie created TOMS, a company that would match every pair of shoes purchased with a pair of new shoes given to a child in need. They state 'With every product you purchase, TOMS will help a person in need.'[61]

Guerrilla Working is the deliberate mixing up of people and teams, bringing talent together wherever it matters to solve issues and create opportunities. It is vital if people are to perform in such circumstances that they are confident in their reason for corporate being and comfortable that they are supported in such ventures.

I have covered some of the more obvious ground rules in an earlier chapter such as the hours in which work is permitted; how to keep in touch; how often an employee is expected to attend meetings and; how to report sickness absence. Yet there are other things to consider, things which are harder to measure.

These will include the readiness of a colleague to work away from their base and indeed the readiness of a manager to let go. Guerrilla Working is not for everyone. Not all of us are able to leave our desks or workstations behind and head out into the jungle in search of adventure and not everyone wants to.

Some people like the comfort of regularity. They like to come to work at the same place every day, park in the same parking space, have their

---

[61] http://www.toms.co.uk/our-movement/l

lunch at the same and take solace in performing tasks that are comfortably within their ken. All workplaces have them and all workplaces need them. They are the bedrock upon which many businesses are built.

Certain aspects of Guerrilla Working have to rely upon those who have regular habits otherwise how would you get in and amongst them? Gaining an understanding of what people do, how they operate and the interactions within their teams can only take place if they happen to be there. If we are all Guerrilla Working all of the time then relationships would take longer to build. They would not be impossible though.

Remember Guerrilla Working is about showing that truly flexible individual and group working is possible and sustainable. It is about leaving the myth behind that an individual's work is inherently linked to their location. It is about the free movement of talent within and between organisations and using this to create new perceptions, new understandings and new opportunities.

It is not about having everyone wandering about in some form of Brownian motion hoping that everything will work out in the end. It is about integration with purpose to meet the common objectives of the organisations.

The best approach is for those who can and want to engage to be allowed to while encouraging those who would benefit to give it a try. There will always be a cohort of those who do not want to change the way they work. They should be net recipients rather than donors but be careful that they do not become victims. Breaking down barriers is the preferred outcome rather than creating a new elitism.

Managers and supervisors need to learn to let go. They need to trust their teams to be out there doing whatever is needed to move the business forward. The focus needs to be on outcomes rather than the method and this can be a problem for a manager who has come through a traditional hierarchical structure. Why should they change when they have got to where they are by doing what they have done?

Trust is the key but this is easier said than done. Trust is not a logical function. It requires belief at a visceral level.

All organisations have employees that present difficulties for managers. Everyone complains about their manager from time to time. Good workers and good managers can go off the boil due to circumstances changing. It may a problem with their home life, an illness or money problems.

These relationships are going to cause problems for Guerrilla Working. Too much focus is made upon managing bad workers out of the organisation. Yet no one sets out to be a bad worker. (Perhaps some do but it will be a very small number). Only the most perverse of managers would deliberately set out to employ a bad worker. Good workers are made bad. They can be worn down by culture and stifled by bad process.

As Jim Womack, President and Founder of Lean Enterprise Institute, Inc. puts it: 'What I find really fascinating is that when good people (that's you and me) are put in a bad process we often become "bad" like the process – mean spirited, foul mouthed, and even violent. Ask everyone involved what the problem is and they are very likely to blame everyone else – the "crazy" passengers, the "petty bureaucrat" check-in agent, the "authoritarian" security force, the "tight-fisted" airline – rather than step back and think about the process itself and how it could be improved.'[62]

The focus of leadership must be on setting the direction and developing the culture that supports its achievement. The focus on management must be on encouraging positive activities that support the organisation's objectives yet too much time is spent on correcting what went wrong rather than developing what went right.

---

[62] http://www.lean.org/womack/DisplayObject.cfm?o=723

You are not going to trust everyone to be a Guerrilla Worker. Within your team there will be those who instinctively get what you are trying to achieve while there will be those with whom you struggle. The majority of your team will be somewhere in the middle. Your focus needs to be on letting those who will, encouraging those who may and managing those who won't.

Remember the Pareto principle[63] and spend most of your effort on the eighty and not the twenty.

The best thing that a manager or leader can do to embed Guerrilla Working however is to lead by example. The leader must prove that it is not only possible but acceptable. They must encourage behaviour that is in line with the aspiration and check that which is not.

Above all the leader must be consistent in both what they say and what they do. There is no point in extolling the virtues of a more agile approach to work only to lock themselves in their office out of sight. People who are willing to follow will be looking for both verbal and visual clues to be in unison.

Being a Guerrilla Worker and a leader requires you to be highly visible, highly mobile and highly adaptable.

And finally

So there you have it. Guerrilla Working is an approach to work that brings people together to challenge the rules and achieve positive things in a short space of time. It is about passion, speed and low cost. It creates something special out of the ordinary, something daring, exciting and fun.

It is about mixing up the people, involving the best of all of the talents to get stuck in and get back out again before everyone becomes too bogged down.

---

[63] http://en.wikipedia.org/wiki/Vilfredo_Pareto

It is a way of releasing the great ideas that are locked away inside your organisation, the ones that are needed for its future development and prosperity.

Your organisation needs you. Be part of the revolution. Be a Guerrilla Worker.

Some useful stuff

Guerrilla Working is not about documentation, process and procedures. It is about relationships, engagement and trust. Having said that it is important that the ground rules are understood and shared. A protocol allows everyone involved to have a degree of definition. A protocol draws the white lines on the pitch upon which we are playing. Here are some useful policies that can be adopted or adapted for your own use

Suggested agile working protocol

A trawl round the internet reveals many useful documents. The following is based upon the Modern and Flexible Working Operating Protocol developed by Warwickshire County Council.[64]

The protocol is developed to ensure that modern and flexible working follows a consistent approach across the organisation and which can facilitate a more flexible approach to work in order to benefit the customers, staff and the organisation as a whole.

Line managers will make a decision in consultation with each individual team member as to what definition of worker they will be under the protocol. This will be documented in an individual's working agreement.

---

[64] http://apps.warwickshire.gov.uk/api/documents/WCCC-575-43

The following role definitions will be used:

Flexible Worker - A flexible worker is someone who can work from a variety of locations for all or part of their working hours in agreement with their manager. For instance they may be able to work from any desk within the organisation, customer's premises, partner premises, home or out in the field.

Office Worker - An office worker is someone who is based in the same location for all of their working hours but may share office space/workstation within a team location in that building.

Fixed Desk Worker - A fixed desk worker is someone who has to work at a fixed desk for all of their working hours. This may be because of equality/disability issues (e.g. specific chair, desk), specific software on PC or specific role.

Work locations may vary according to service needs. Where home is deemed part of the working location the following definitions may also apply. These can be mixed with role definitions and are not mutually exclusive.

Contracted Home Worker – A contracted home worker is someone who has a formal arrangement in place to work all or part of their working hours at home, as stated in their contract of employment.

Regular Home Worker – A regular home worker who regularly works at home on a non-contractual basis but they have a formal arrangement with their manager whereby they work at home for least one working day each week.

Occasional Home Worker - An occasional home worker is someone who works at home on an ad hoc, occasional or informal basis during their normal working hours e.g. to write a specific report.

The main requirement of managing modern and flexible working is to manage results or outcomes rather than the process. Line managers and staff will agree how individual performance is to be monitored when creating an individual's working agreement. Objectives will be agreed at individual sessions in line with a supportive management approach. Managers will not normally need to be prescriptive about how the objectives are achieved.

Individual one-to-one sessions will be held on a regular basis between staff and their line manager. Attendance is obligatory and they will be held at the most appropriate location for the individual and their line manager.

Work outcomes will be managed at the individual sessions between managers and their staff. These will include a review of work load and time management with emphasis on what is going well and how this can be applied to those areas that may be going less well. It will be the joint responsibility between the line manager and the employee to discuss and agree clear and tangible objectives with suitable outcomes and realistic performance measures achievable within the individual's working hours.

Service delivery hours will vary across the organisation and teams will need to be aware of public access times and service demands. Teams will need to decide how their working arrangements will be made in order to meet the requirements of the service and its customers. Consideration should be given to customer needs, duty cover and emergency contacts where required. It will be the responsibility of the manager to manage levels of cover required to meet their service standards. Special arrangements may apply during holiday periods, adverse weather and emergency situations. Such arrangements at times may be at odds with a truly flexible and agile workforce and all employees will be expected, where reasonable, to put the needs of the service delivery first.

For most roles there will be a requirement for staff to interact with a range of colleagues in their own and other functions and departments. Where this is the case flexible working arrangements must reflect the

.

organisation's main hours of work, say from 8 am to 6 pm Monday to Friday and there is an expectation that staff will be available for the majority of their work day during these times.

There is an expectation that all employees will be required to spend some of their working time with colleagues or customers. The actual amount of time that a flexible or mobile worker will be expected to be present in the office may vary and will depend on the agreed role. This will form part of the discussion when creating an individual's working agreement. All employees will be expected to remain flexible, where reasonable and attend meetings, training and seminars etc. at locations required by the organisation.

Flexible working arrangements will play an important role in helping to manage peaks and troughs in terms of service delivery. This will form part of the normal planning process that recognises the cyclical nature of the business and the manageable workload will be agreed in advance taking into account the needs of the service. Wherever possible the needs of the individual will be taken into account and the allocation of work will need to be consistent and fair. In times of high and unexpected demand all employees are expected to remain flexible where reasonable.

All individuals are responsible for making themselves available during their agreed working hours and accounting for their time to ensure workload is manageable. In some circumstances timesheets will be required, for example when work is directly chargeable. Where this is the case it is the individual's responsibility to complete these timesheets accurately.

All employees should take a sensible approach to managing their work time and give due regard to their health, safety and well-being while working flexibly. For example there is a legal requirement to have a minimum of 20 minute break after 6 hours of continuous work and lunch breaks should be taken at a reasonable time. Flexible working arrangements should not be used as a way of avoiding healthy working practices.

If an individual is unable to work because of sickness, they must follow the organisation's sickness absence management procedure. If an individual is sick then they are not expected to work.

In normal circumstances, flexible working arrangements are not a substitute for childcare or other dependent care requirements. When an employee is at work then they cannot be expected to perform caring duties at the same time.

Being in contact is a critical requirement to ensuring successful flexible working arrangements. Working beyond normal office boundaries will require flexible and mobile workers to make greater use of technology to remain in-touch. The appropriate communications channels will be agreed as part of the individual's working agreement and will include such tools as email, mobile phone and instant messaging or online chat. Individuals will have a preference for one channel over another and agreement should be reached during the individual sessions between managers and their staff.

Everyone should be contactable when they are working regardless of their physical working location. Where a work mobile phone has been issued this should be on when an individual is working. It should be put on silent mode when an individual is in a meeting or unable to answer and checked regularly.

It is the responsibility of all employees to ensure arrangements are in place to allow colleagues and customers to contact them. Calendars should be open to all employees and private meetings marked as such. Where instant messaging or online chat is used then all employees should log in and set an appropriate status during their agreed hours of work.

Attendance at some meetings will be mandatory. Notes will be taken at team meetings to share with those unable to attend because of leave or other absence. If invited to attend a meeting there is the expectation that employees will make every reasonable effort to accommodate that request unless there is a business reason which prevents the individual from doing so.

The measures taken to protect information when working outside the office should be at least as stringent as those taken in the office. All employees are required to understand their responsibilities associated with the security of the equipment they use, and any information they have access to. Extra vigilance will be required when employees are away from their normal environment and should ensure that they carry with them only that documentation required during that period. Staff will be expected to comply with the organisations information security policies and procedures.

Equipment, training and procedural requirements required to comply with the Information Security policies will be discussed and implemented as part of the individual's working arrangements.

Suggested clear workspace protocol

Guerrilla Working is about getting in and amongst your colleagues and customers, creating new experiences, new perspectives and new relationships. It's one thing turning up and starting work from whichever location you happen to park yourself at but if your organisation really wants to embrace different and flexible ways of working then it has to make the workspace open and inviting.

What is needed is a clear workspace protocol. This is not just a clear desk policy though that is part of the deal. It is about the whole office or work environment.

The following is based on policies and protocols developed by Registers of Scotland[65] and PrivacySense.[66]

The protocol is developed to ensure that the workplace assets of the

---

[65] http://www.ros.gov.uk/public/about_us./foi/sia/clear_desk_policy.html
[66] http://www.privacysense.net/clear-desk-policy/

organisation are left in a clean and acceptable way at the end of a working period to facilitate a more flexible approach to work in order to benefit the customers, staff and the organisation as a whole.

The benefits of clear workspace protocol are that it:

- Improves the use of organisational assets. The workspace should be seen as an asset of the organisation rather than the residence of the individual. Territorial claiming and over-personalisation should be discouraged in order that all workspaces can be available for other workers and colleagues to use.
- Saves Time and Money. Making more of the organisation's assets available will result in requiring less of them. The use of workspace assets can be maximised leading to a reduced capital investment and ongoing revenue costs. A clear workspace will ensure that important documentation, for example can be found by other employees.
- Creates good impressions. First impressions can be lasting and one of the best ways to create an impression that your work place is inefficient and disorganised is to have the workspaces a mess. Having a clear workspace protocol ensures that all employees understand the role of the work place in enhancing the organisation's brand, especially when customers are involved.
- Improves security. Sensitive information is often left on desks. Reports, minutes and Post-it notes containing names, phone numbers, and even user names and passwords are left visible in plain view. The protocol ensures that good security practice is maintained so that employees and visitors do not have access to information they should not see. This reduces the chance of an information security incident resulting in financial and reputational damage.
- Reduces Stress. When employees are organized they can spend more time concentrating on work rather than stressing out

because they are unable to find the tools or information that they require.

- Improves health and safety. Having a tidy workspace will lead to less likelihood of accidents occurring. Creating a safe working environment is one of the key responsibilities of management and a clear workspace protocol supports this.
- Shows respect. Ensuring that your employees tidy up after themselves and leave the workspace in a way that others can enjoy working in shows respect for the organisation, their fellow workers and its customers.

In order to comply with the clear workspace protocol, at the end of a daily work period all employees must:

- Clear their desk and the surrounding workspace of all documentation and information whether it is in electronic or hard copy format. This should either be stored in:
  o The personal storage provided for hard copy documentation.
  o Common storage for shared files of hard copy documentation.
  o Personal or shared areas for electronic document storage. Documents open in work sharing applications such as SharePoint should be checked in.
  o Or:
  o Placed in the post tray, clearly labelled for onward distribution.
  o Disposed of securely using the organisation's agreed disposal method.
- Put away any tools or equipment that have been used.
- Replace the furniture to as it was found.
- Switch off desktop computers if appropriate.
- Remove any personalisation.

It should be noted that some personalisation may be permitted. In some organisations workspaces can be classified depending upon the type of person who is most likely to work there. At O2's head office in Slough they define their employees as either huggers or hoppers. Huggers predominantly come into the office on a daily basis and so are permitted to occupy the same workspace or one within the same area. Hoppers are people who are more agile and are able to occupy any of the workspaces that are designated for their use and have not been reserved for that period. Huggers are allowed a certain but limited amount of personalisation. Items such as photographs, soft toys and pot plants are allowed but restricted in their quantity.

The clear workspace protocol should be adopted by all employees and it is essential that senior management lead by example. If anything, senior management should have even more clear workspaces than those who look to them for leadership.

To make the clear workspace protocol work effectively there are several things that are required to be in place. Most of these have been referred to within the description above.

Personal storage: If paperwork is not to be left on desks and jackets left on the backs of chairs then adequate space must be made available for people to store their belongings. Sufficient coat hangers and lockers should be provided. The latter need to be lockable and may need to contain paperwork as well as personal belongings.

Group storage: Those items that are for shared use need to be borrowed and returned to some group storage areas. Again these will need to be able to accommodate whatever is needed to conduct the business of the organisation and need to be lockable for when the building is unoccupied. Consideration needs to be given to the system for removing and returning documentation in order to track its location as well as who is responsible for the security of assets and information.

Document retention and destruction policies: Paper and electronic document management play an important role in maintaining clear workspaces. Clear guidance on how to store documents, when to get rid of them and how to do so in a secure manner are required.

Suggested lone worker protocol

Guerrilla Working is about getting in and amongst your colleagues and customers. You may find yourself in places that you don't normally frequent. I've already covered this in the section on staying safe but a useful addition to improving the welfare of staff who are out and about is through a lone worker protocol. The following is based upon work carried out by the NHS Employers Organisation.[67]

Lone workers don't need to be alone, in fact they rarely are. They are often in with clients and can be vulnerable and at increased risk of physical or verbal abuse and harassment from other employees and customers simply because they don't have the immediate support of their team members. They are also at increased risk from injury through accidents as colleagues are not there to look out for them.

The protocol helps employers, managers and staff deal with the important issue of staff working on their own, and in particular to stress the need for robust risk assessment and risk management in lone worker situations.

The Health and Safety Executive (HSE) defines lone workers as 'those who work by themselves without close or direct supervision'[68] and lists a number of examples including those who:

- Work from a fixed base, such as one person working alone on a premises (for example estates staff).
- Work separately from others on the same premises (for example security staff) or outside normal hours (for example on-call staff).

---

[67]

http://www.nhsemployers.org/Aboutus/Publications/Documents/Lone%20working.pdf

[68] Working alone in safety: controlling the risks of solitary work, HSE, 1998

- Work away from a fixed base.
- Work at home.
- Mobile workers.

Lone working does not automatically mean a higher risk of violence, but it is generally understood that it does increase workers' vulnerability. This vulnerability will depend on the type of situation in which the lone work is being carried out.

It is important that each organisation gives definition to its understanding of what lone working is. In the example that I have based this protocol on the NHS Security Management Service defines lone working as: 'Any situation or location in which someone works without a colleague nearby; or when someone is working out of sight or earshot of another colleague'.

This widens the notional concept of a lone worker to encompass many roles that exist within our own workplace. Rather than being a person who is working in a client's house, such as a social worker, or a technician providing a service in some remote location, such as a telephone engineer up a pole alongside a country road. A lone worker could be any of us. In fact it is likely that all of us will find ourselves in lone working situations almost on a daily basis.

Guerrilla Working however increase the likelihood of colleagues working in such situations.

The risks of lone working can be mitigated by addressing the five following areas:

- Risk assessment. Ensuring that proper assessment is made of the likely risks that a lone worker could face and implementing mitigation.
- Prevention. The most effective way to reduce the risks to lone workers is to prevent them from finding themselves in such

situations. This is not always possible yet consideration can be given as to whether alternative approaches exist.

- Policy. A strong lone worker policy should be introduced and complied with.
- Training should be made available to all employees on how to manage themselves when lone working.
- Support from the employer. Willing and ready support from management and colleagues will give confidence to lone workers that they are being looked out for.

Support from the employer can come in many guises including:

- Providing information to help workers assess risks and ensure safety.
- Investing in technology and services that help staff to summon help discreetly.
- Provide training for example on conflict management.

All individuals within an organisation have a duty of care to their colleagues. Everyone is equal but some are more equal than others. In ensuring that a lone worker protocol is effective there are certain roles that play a greater part.

Senior management must set the tone and support the development and embedding of appropriate policies and procedures. As already described, nearly all people will find then themselves as a lone worker from time to time and they will be included. These situations will allow them to demonstrate that the policies apply to the whole organisation.

The Human Resources team, assuming that there is one, will be responsible for developing the policies and ensuring that they remain up to date and relevant. They should ensure that these are disseminated to all relevant staff including those responsible for their implementation and those whom they are designed to safeguard.

Such local policies and procedures should always be developed in consultation with relevant stakeholders. These include health and safety advisers, line managers, risk managers and staff representatives such as trade unions and professional bodies.

Human Resources should also take the lead in investigating when a breach of any policy takes place. They should work with line managers to ensure that appropriate remedial measures are taken and that lessons are learnt. Findings from these investigations should be used to shape amendments to future policies and procedures.

The line manager has a responsibility to ensure that all relevant policies and procedures are implemented and disseminated to lone working staff they are responsible for. They must ensure that they are appropriately protected before finding themselves in a lone working situation.

This includes ensuring that a suitable and sufficient risk assessment is conducted in consultation with the appropriate people to ensure that all risks from lone working are identified and appropriate control measures introduced to minimise, control or remove them.

These control measures will include ensuring that lone workers receive sufficient information, training, instruction and advice. The line manager must also ensure that any necessary physical measures are put in place, appropriate technology is made available and, where the safety of lone workers is threatened, that alternative arrangements can be made.

Line manages should also ensure that relevant policies are embedded in the day to day activities of their team and that any breaches are evidenced, recorded and reported properly.

Individual workers have a responsibility to take reasonable care of themselves and to cooperate with their employer under health and safety legislation. They need to make full use of any training, technology, equipment and advice from their line managers regarding lone working.

Employees should plan their work appropriately to understand any risk they may face and take necessary action to minimise the possibility of an incident occurring.

No employee should put themselves at risk. If a situation arises that they are unfamiliar with or in which they feel unsafe, they should withdraw and seek further advice and assistance.

If there is a breach of the lone worker policy then the employee involved has a responsibility to record and report it properly so that lessons can be learnt.

The risk assessment process relies on using all available information in relation to lone working to ensure that the risk of future incidents can be minimised. This includes learning from operational experience of previous incidents and involving feedback from all parties. All employees should be encouraged to report identified risks to managers, as well as near misses, so that a risk assessment can be carried out, appropriate action taken and mitigations put in place.

The risk assessment should consider:

- Lone working staff groups exposed to risk due to working in abnormal and hazardous conditions.
- Particular work activities that might present a risk to lone workers.
- Staff delivering unwelcome information or bad news.
- The possibility of an increased risk of violence from service users.
- Those working in or travelling between certain environments or settings.
- Lone workers carrying equipment that makes them a target for theft or less able to protect themselves.
- An evaluation of capability to undertake lone working, for example being inexperienced or having a disability.

The following factors need to be addressed:

- Type of incident risk such as increased risk of injury.
- Likelihood or frequency of incident.
- Likely severity of the incident.
- Control measures in place.
- Actions needed to mitigate.

An assessment of known risks and mitigations should be kept. This should be shared with all relevant staff who may find themselves in a similar lone worker situation. Such an assessment may include personal and confidential information and so consideration needs to be given as to how this information will be shared.

Where a High-risk activity is identified then lone working should not be permitted and any employee should be accompanied by an appropriate colleague. This can include work in specific locations, conditions and with certain individuals.

Personal equipment that will improve the safety and welfare of a lone worker, such as a mobile phone should be maintained in good working order and checked regularly.

Lone workers should always ensure that someone else, preferably their line manager is aware of their movements. Maintaining an accurate and open calendar showing the address of where they will be working, details of the people they will be working with or visiting and telephone numbers should suffice.

Lone workers and their line manager or relevant colleague should remain in regular contact particularly if there plans have changed. Where there is genuine concern, as a result of a lone worker failing to attend a visit or an arranged meeting within an agreed time, or to make contact as agreed, the line manager should attempt to locate them and check that they are safe. If it is thought that the lone worker may be at risk, it is important that matters are dealt with quickly, after considering all the available facts.

As an alternative to line managers keeping regular contact with lone workers which may not always be practical a buddy system could be used. Here each lone worker nominates a buddy who will:

- Be fully aware of the movements of the lone worker.
- Have all necessary contact details for the lone worker.
- Have details of the lone worker's plans.
- Keep in regular contact with the lone worker.
- Follow the agreed escalation procedures should they have concerns.

For the buddy system to work effectively then the buddy must be made aware that they have been nominated and the procedures and requirement for this role as well as any contingency arrangements should they be unable to fulfil the role.

Lone workers should be able, through appropriate training, to recognise the risk to themselves and be alert to any warning signs. They should be in a position to make a personal risk assessment and take appropriate action including not carrying on their work. At no point should a lone worker place themselves in danger.

About the author

Phil Jackman is Head of ICT Services at Durham County Council in the North East of England. He has worked in the ICT industry for over twenty years in both the private and public sectors. Prior to that he worked in logistics and distribution. He chairs the North East ICT Managers group and Society of ICT Managers North East. He is an advisory board member of Dynamo North East, an organisation dedicated to growing the ICT economy across the region.

www.ingramcontent.com/pod-product-compliance
Lightning Source LLC
Chambersburg PA
CBHW051908170526
45168CB00001B/295